The Student Guide to

BTEC

Design

Norman Lucking
Colchester Institute

Series Editor: **Alan Kitson**
Bolton Institute of Higher Education

MACMILLAN

First edition 1991

Published by
MACMILLAN EDUCATION LTD
Houndmills, Basingstoke, Hampshire RG21 2XS
and London
Companies and representatives throughout the world

Printed in Hong Kong

British Library Cataloguing in Publication Data
Lucking, Norman
The Student Guide to BTEC design.–(The Student Guide to BTEC).
1. Great Britain. Higher education institutions.
Curriculum subjects: Design
I. Title   II. Series
745.4071141
ISBN 0–333–51730–X

Contents

Acknowledgements

The author and publisher wish to thank the following for permission to use copyright material: Business & Technician Education Council; Colchester Institute; Croydon College; The Design Council; Medway College; Rycotewood College; Pam Schomberg; U.C.C. International Group Ltd.

Every effort has been made to trace copyright holders, but if any have been inadvertently overlooked the publishers will be pleased to make the necessary arrangements at the first opportunity.

UNIT 1 How to use this book

In this unit you will:

- find out what is in this book;
- learn how to use the book;
- find out how it can help you in your studies.

Introduction

'Designer' is a word you see everywhere today. There are designer clothes, designer labels and even designer foods. There are also fashion designers, engineering designers, industrial designers, textile designers, graphic designers, furniture designers, packaging designers and interior designers. There are designers who design products, designers who design systems and designers who design environments. It is no wonder, therefore, that many people are confused about what a designer actually is and does.

When you try to find simple definitions for 'designer' and 'design' they are usually very general, dictionary-type definitions. A typical example of this would be: 'A designer is one who plans and shapes an artefact, system or environment.' This makes all of us designers whenever we consciously change something or solve a problem. It does not help those who have heard that there are careers in design and want to find out what designers actually do, what skills, knowledge and qualities are needed to be a designer, what design courses have to offer and what the career opportunities are.

This book will not attempt to define 'designer' or 'design' in a few, simple, all-embracing words. It will aim to help you analyse what designers do and why they do it, by looking at *what* is learnt on BTEC design courses, *how* you can learn about design and *why* you have to learn such things. It is not a 'magic' book and it will not make you a great designer, because designing takes a lot of hard work and you only learn to design through the experience of designing. What this book will do, however, is make you more aware of design, give you the opportunity to experience designing for yourself, generally prepare you for studying a BTEC National level design course and help you with such studies.

This book is obviously most useful to those of you who have already been selected to join a BTEC National level design course. But those who are just interested in the subject, are considering design as a career or are wondering what you need to do or know in order to be selected for a design course, will also find the book relevant.

What will I find in this book?

You will already have noticed that the book is divided into *units* instead of chapters. Each *unit* has a *title*, identifying as concisely as possible what is covered in the section, followed by a box containing a list of *aims*. These aims will help you to understand what we expect you to achieve through studying the unit. All BTEC courses have to produce a similar list of aims for each subject studied on the course programme.

Activity 1

We could tell you about the content of the book by giving you a list of unit numbers and titles. This would tell you what is in the book and where you could find information, but it would not show you how to use the book or make you aware of its usefulness. You must find out these things for yourself. This activity will help you to decide how the book can help you, which parts will be most useful and where such information can be found.

- Try to think of the things you would like to know about design and the BTEC design courses. Make a list of these.

- Look through the book, concentrating on the aims box at the start of each unit, to see whether any section has information that relates to the things on your list.

- Make a note of the units you think will be especially useful.

You will note that in Activity 1 we have asked you to find things out for yourself, rather than just tell you about them. This is important, because it illustrates the way you will be expected to learn about things on a BTEC course. On design courses you will not sit in a classroom and be taught art and design, you will do *projects* which will ask you to find things out and learn ways to do things by actually doing them.

Doing *projects* is not just the way that BTEC design students learn, it is a common method of learning for all BTEC students. In other subjects, however, projects may be referred to as *assignments, programme of integrative assignments* or even *PIAs*.

Most design skills and information you will find out about and develop by experience. You will try things out for yourself, you will discover what information is useful and where you can get it. And you will actually have to use this information or these skills in the way that you would use them in a job.

You will find that learning in this way is not only useful while you are at college and doing a BTEC course, it also continues to be useful when you have left college and have a job. You will find yourself gradually becoming less reliant on your lecturers and being able to learn for yourself, a skill that continues to be useful as you get older and need to change or adapt to different technology or attitudes. You will find that some things change so quickly that they are out of date within a very short time. Knowing about such things could, therefore, inhibit your design ability and it may be more important to be able to know where and how to get up-to-date information.

Summary

This book is like a BTEC design course. It has *units* which represent the different sections of information we feel you need. It has *aims* which list what we expect you to learn from reading and doing each unit. And it has *activities* which will ask you to find things out for yourself and use this information. By doing these activities you will be prepared for the way you will have to work on BTEC design courses, and you will also develop some of the skills you will need.

You will also find that some of the activities build up into *projects* which are not so defined as activities, and present more opportunities for individual interests to be developed.

To get maximum benefit from this book you must do some, if not all, of the projects and activities. Do not be afraid of making mistakes or having your ideas criticised, because learning about design is about building on mistakes and getting experience. No designer gets it right first time or is successful every time. In fact, the irritating thing about design is that there are no right and wrong answers, just better and worse ones. What you must do, however, is commit yourself, produce words, drawings or objects, so that people can see your ideas, comment on them and suggest improvements. Designing is not a natural talent, it has to be developed and you have to work hard at it.

UNIT 2

Are you going to be a successful BTEC design student?

Will you be able to cope with the way of working on a BTEC design course? What standards of work will be expected of you? How will you compare with the other students on the course?

In this unit you will:

- analyse what skills, knowledge and qualities you already have;

- understand what qualities interviewers look for when selecting students;

- understand why they look for such qualities;

- find out what BTEC design courses do.

BTEC design courses and college life in general are different in many ways from life at school. You will already have done some project or course work as part of the GCSE programme. You will have some experience of working on your own or with others, of finding things out for yourself, of problem solving and organising your time to finish within deadlines. But college is still different and you must expect to adapt yourself and the way you work to suit such change.

How is college different to school?

Unlike school, college is not compulsory and when you study on a BTEC course you are expected to be committed to such study. Students who do not show commitment could be considered as unsuitable and asked to leave or reconsider their choice of career. Colleges will encourage those who try but are harsh with those who waste time. This is especially the case on design courses, because many of the tutors are professional designers and they know that designers are only successful if they work hard. Talent is not, by itself, enough.

You will have changed from studying a selection of subjects to a more limited range, chosen by the college to prepare you for a job in design. Some BTEC design courses, such as General Art and Design, have options which introduce a range of design careers, but most courses are composed of pre-selected subjects. You will have to pass all the subjects on the course to be awarded a BTEC National Diploma or Certificate. Some of these you may be good at, and get a distinction grade in, others you may not be so good at. You cannot leave any out, however, and you must complete each subject to a satisfactory level.

The GCSE subjects that you studied at school placed a lot of emphasis on projects or course work. This will have prepared you for the projects on which BTEC design students are asked to work. At school, each subject usually has its own course work, but on a BTEC design course most of the subjects share a common project. This form of shared project is known as *integrative assignments*. If such a shared project is structured well, the individual subjects will blend together to such an extent that it will be difficult to identify each specific subject. This may be confusing at first, especially if you are concerned with getting good grades for individual subjects. Do not worry. The assessment of the projects takes this into account and the blending of the subjects in a relevant way is considered especially important.

College will sometimes appear to be more relaxed and less demanding than school. When working on projects most students use the design studio only as a base. Although you do most of your design work here, you will also be going out to find information or attend lectures in other parts of the college. You will be managing your own time and are encouraged to spend some of your time discussing work with colleagues.

Less guidance and control from teachers does not mean that BTEC design course work is less demanding. If you want a career in design it is not enough to be satisfactory or work just to achieve a pass. Your Diploma or Certificate will have to be supported by a good portfolio of work, which you will show to employers or a college of higher education to get you a job or be accepted onto another course.

You will have to set your own standards and work hard to achieve them, if you want to succeed in a design career. These standards will not only be determined by your particular class or year group at college, but by design students nationally – students with whom you will be competing for jobs or places on higher level courses. You will have to combine creative talent with hard work, and may find yourself doing what most other design students do – spending many extra hours working on your projects. This may mean working longer hours that most of the other students in the college.

Can you cope?

BTEC courses represent the transition between the worlds of school and work. They develop the concept of a broad education and the learning of many unrelated subjects to a more structured programme of related subjects, selected to prepare you for the specific job or career you want.

You are probably not too concerned just yet about how you will learn the skills and find the knowledge needed to get a job. You are probably more concerned about whether you will be able to cope with the work you will be asked to do on your BTEC design course. You may be anxious about the standard of work that will be expected of you, and wondering how you will compare with your colleagues.

One thing you must remember is that you are only on a course because you have been considered good enough not only to complete the course but also to be a designer. BTEC design courses are very closely monitored, and there are people called Moderators who regularly visit colleges to ensure that all students meet the required level of entry and show the necessary potential for a career in design.

Because you are on a design course, and design courses usually have many applicants, you will already have been through a stringent selection system. This not only looks at your academic achievements, such as the number and grades of your GCSE passes, but also your design ability and character. Design courses look for those students who are not only good at exams, but who are good at designing, are committed to the subject and can express themselves confidently.

You will probably have had an interview at which you presented your work and were asked to talk about it. You will also have been asked to talk about yourself, explaining why you wanted to be a designer, why you chose that specific design course and how you thought your career might develop. You would also have been asked about how you went about designing, what your general interests were and how much designing you did outside of school hours.

The staff who interviewed you are specialists in teaching design and they know what to look for in potential design students. Because they have had experience of hundreds of students before you, they know not only what skills you need but also what type of person is best suited to a career in design. They would have applied these criteria to each student interviewed.

If you survived such a selection procedure and have satisfied the staff who will teach you that you have potential, you should not only complete the course but be able to progress to employment or higher education. You *will* be able to cope.

If you have not already thought about your interview and analysed your strengths and weaknesses or where you did well or badly, it may be worth doing this now. BTEC courses not only teach new skills and give you new facts, they also develop the skills you already have. Understanding your own potential will help this process.

Activity 2

- Make a list of the skills you think a good designer needs and the things she or he has to know about.

- Look back on your interview and review your own portfolio. Where do you think you did well or badly? What are your strengths and weaknesses?

- Write a short review of your potential and show examples of work which support this.

- If you have not yet had an interview, think about what might be expected and assess the work in your portfolio.

- Pick out your best piece of work and explain why you think it is important for the interviewers to consider it.

- Compare your assessment and review with the points considered in the following section.

How design students are selected

Different colleges and different design courses ask for different things to be shown at interview.. General Art and Design courses may ask to see a wide variety of experimental art and design work, for example, whereas a more specialised course, like Industrial Design, may prefer to see CDT as well as art and design work. Generally, however, although the work in the portfolio may be different, your interviewers would have reviewed it – and you – in similar ways and looked for similar things, such as:

- drawing ability
- creativity
- visual judgement

- commitment to becoming a designer
- presentation and self-marketing skills
- design awareness

Drawing ability

Designers are expected to be able to draw. It is this activity above all others that people associate with art and design and use as their criteria for judging whether a designer is competent or not. It is, however, more than a trade skill of the designer – it is a very useful activity and helps the designer in many ways.

Primarily drawing is a form of communication. It helps the designer to explain complex ideas in an effective way. To say that a drawing is worth a hundred or even a thousand words would be devaluing its true worth. Designers need to have their ideas and designs understood in order that these can be accepted, produced, financed, commented on and improved. It is essential that the form of communication designers use stimulates such responses.

It is not only other people designers need to communicate with – they also need a method of getting ideas out of their own heads, of realising and visualising ideas. Good drawing skills help to do this by generating confidence, stimulating comment and encouraging idea development. As you get better at drawing and find it easier to put your ideas into pictures, so you will be more self-critical and your ideas will develop and change. Such development is necessary, because designers seldom come up with good ideas straight away. They try different ideas, build on them, discard, modify and improve them. You will need to draw well enough to concentrate more on the actual design than on how you are drawing it.

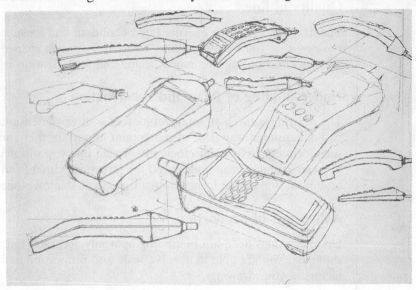

Drawing is also part of the creative process. A good designer 'thinks' with the pencil, because putting down marks stimulates more and more ideas, both from other people and yourself.

Finally, designers expect other designers to draw. It is the craft skill that every designer appreciates, considers to be important and looks for in other designers. It is one of the major assets you will have when trying to get a job in design. It make your immediately useful and commercially viable.

What makes a good drawing?

Quality of line

The drawing should be executed in a confident and sensitive manner, showing that you have the ability to create, through changes of pressure and thickness of line, the mood, shape and form of what is being drawn.

Understanding of form and construction

The drawing is often an interpretation of a three-dimensional form in a two-dimensional way. It is of paramount important that you can define such form effectively and efficiently. To do this you will need to show that you can explore form, understand the structure within form and the space around it, and define form through the use of shadow, tone and texture.

Awareness of proportion

Good drawings need not be photographically accurate, but it is essential to show that you are able to observe scale and proportion and re-create such factors in your drawings.

Composition

The way pictures are drawn, the position of the drawing on the page and the relationship of one drawing to another are all important, because they help to create a 'designerly' image. You should not just be concerned with the drawing alone, therefore, but relate it to the space and other drawings around it, creating an interesting, stimulating and harmonious total effect.

Effective use of medium

Drawings need not only be in pencil. Staff on design courses like to see that students have explored the use of other mark-making materials, such as charcoal, pastels, ink or marker pens.

Evidence of observation

Drawing is a rigorous activity and you need to show that you have really looked at whatever you are drawing and have tried to understand it and define it. You must also show that you have understood some of the basic rules used in drawing such as perspective or angles of ellipses.

Evidence of enquiry

Drawing is a form of exploration, and you should show that you can use it to explore and record ideas, forms, shapes and emotions.

Creativity

Designers are expected to be creative people, and your interviewers will have been looking at how many ideas you had, what sort of ideas they were, how original and how visually exciting they were. Many design specialism interviewers would have expected to have seen some GCSE project work or course work that showed, through the use of sketch sheets, how you thought of ideas, developed them, modified them and selected them for presentation. Just by looking at such work they could also see how organised you are, how logical you are, whether you are able to express ideas and whether you are aware of the criteria for good design.

Visual judgement

Whatever design specialism you wish to study, you will be expected to show an appreciation of good form, have a sense of colour, an eye for detail and an awareness of contemporary design and fashion. All these things can be assessed by looking at the work in your portfolio. They can be seen not only in the way you execute a particular drawing, but by the way you compose sketches on your sketch sheets, lay out presentation sheets, write explanations and even the way you package your work.

Commitment to becoming a designer

However talented you might be, the design profession cannot afford too many 'prima donnas'. The job of design has to be worthy of the fee it commands and designers have to work hard to get their ideas accepted by other people, some of whom do not appreciate aesthetics to the same degree. The selection panel would have expected to see examples of work that showed your commitment to design. They would not have been content with just being shown a few examples of work that you had been set at school, but also the extra work you undertook out of school in your own time. They would have looked at the quantity of work you had produced, the degree to which you had worked on a piece to get it 'right' and the amount of visual research you had undertaken through the use of sketch and scrap books.

Presentation and self-marketing skills

The way you look, talk and present your work is extremely important to the professional designer. As we have said before, the people whom designers often have to persuade, to get their designs accepted for development and production, do not always have the same degree of visual awareness as the designer. Such people cannot rely on their own expertise but expect the designer to generate enthusiasm and confidence. Your interviewers probably questioned you about your work and your attitude to design to see if you could talk fluently and with the necessary degree of conviction and enthusiasm that generates confidence.

Design awareness

Because design is not just a job but a career and a way of life, it is not the kind of profession you just drift into. Your interviewers would have been anxious to see how much homework about the course and design in general you had done before applying for selection. You will probably have been questioned on why you wanted to study design, what sort of designing appealed to you and whether you had found out about the work of any professional designer.

How will you compare with other students?

You might have found that the interviewers and selection panel interpreted your work in a different way to your GCSE examiners and your teachers. You might have thought that your work was better or worse than that of other people in your class at school who were either accepted for the same course or who failed to get on to the course. Do not forget, however, that the selection panel and interviewers were not only assessing your work they were also assessing *you*, the complete person. They were looking for students who had potential and would respond to their teaching and the course learning programme.

Activity 3

- Try to find out more about the other students on your course.

- Discuss each other's interviews with them and look at each other's portfolios of work.

- Decide, using the selection criteria as a guide, whether all of you fulfilled the points that we have identified.

- Decide on each other's strengths and weaknesses.

- Think about what you may need to do to develop your strengths and improve your weaknesses.

Most course selection panels try very hard to get a group of students together who have a range of different strengths and weaknesses as well as different interests. This is because project work allows you to learn from each other as well as from the lecturers. You will find this variety valuable for establishing standards in your group, creating objectives to work to and promoting visual stimulus or comment. You will also discover that, because you are different, there will be many different answers to the problems you are asked to solve. This will broaden your outlook on design and stimulate a higher degree of creativity than if you were all the same.

Summary

By undertaking the activities in this unit and analysing what we have told you about design and the criteria for selecting students you should:

- be more aware that you have already been through a rigorous selection procedure;
- be more confident that your interviewers have decided that you have the potential to complete the course successfully;
- be more aware that design is not just about drawing and that other skills are needed to make a successful designer;
- be more aware of the skills, strengths and weaknesses of your colleagues.

It is hoped that by being aware of these factors you will feel more confident in undertaking the course, producing work, and generating the necessary criticism to stimulate creativity and learning.

Do not be afraid of making mistakes. The more you do, the more response you will get and the more you will learn.

UNIT 3 Career possibilities

What sort of jobs are available in design? What sort of job would suit you? What sort of BTEC design course will train you for the career of your choice?

In this unit you will:

- become more aware of the range of different design specialisms and job opportunities that are available;

- develop through this awareness a direction to your study which will stimulate further commitment.

Most of you reading this book will already be on a BTEC National level course and will probably have looked at the career opportunities that are open to you when you have successfully completed your studies. Others may be using this book to find out more about design and BTEC design courses before deciding on a career or a course in further education. In either case it is important that you are aware of the scope of design job opportunities available and where your interests can be directed. It is also important to realise that, whatever design course you are on, whether it be a specialist or a general course, much of the content will be applicable to many design disciplines and you will have the opportunity to select with more understanding and authority later.

There are two main types of BTEC design courses at National level, the *general design course* and the *specialist design course*. Of these the BTEC General Art and Design course, often known as GAD, is the most common, and is to be found in most colleges which have an art and design department. General Art and Design courses are structured to introduce you to the different areas of design, as well as to develop those skills and ways of thinking common to all design disciplines.

You are usually introduced to these different areas by undertaking a short project in each, and then having the opportunity to study those you like most by selecting them as options as the course develops. Most of these courses assume that the most likely outlet for students is higher education, rather than direct into industry or the design profession.

Specialist courses are designed to qualify students for jobs as well as for studying in higher education, and, therefore, there is not the same scope for trying out such a broad range of options. Even in these specialist courses, however, there is a concentration on introducing and developing a range of skills which are important to *all* design specialisms, and projects are often structured so that you can tailor them to suit your own individual needs. This means that, even if you have studied on a BTEC National Diploma (Furniture), you could still be able to change to a BTEC Higher National Diploma course or a degree course in, say, Industrial Design, later.

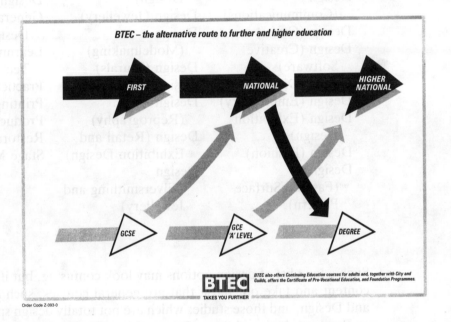

Order Code Z-093-0

Design specialisms

Before we look at the design skills, knowledge and awareness common to all design activities and design jobs, let us look at the range of design specialisms available at BTEC National level, as listed over the page.

Clothing
Conservation and
    Restoration Studies
Design
Design (Advertising)
Design (Architectural
    Stained Glass)
Design (Audio
    Visual)
Design
    (Bookbinding)
Design (Ceramics)
Design
    (Communications)
Design (Crafts)
Design (Creative
    Software)
Design (Display)
Design (Embroidery)
Design (Exhibition
    Design)
Design (Fashion)
Design
    (Fashion/Surface
    Pattern)
Design
    (Fashion/Textiles)
Design (Film and
    Television)
Design (Footwear)
Design (Furniture)
Design (Graphic
    Design)
Design (Illustration)
Design (Industrial
    Design)
Design (Interior
    Design)
Design (Jewellery)
Design
    (Modelmaking)
Design (Murals)
Design (Packaging)
Design
    (Reprography)
Design (Retail and
    Exhibition Design)
Design
    (Silversmithing and
    Jewellery)
Design (Spatial
    Design)
Design (Surface
    Pattern)
Design (Technical
    Illustration)
Design (Textiles)
Design (Theatre
    Studies)
Design
    (Three-dimensional
    Design)
Design (Typography)
General Art and
    Design
Learning Resources
    Technology
Practical Archaeology
Printing
Product Design
Restoration Studies
Stage Management

Such a long list of design options may look confusing, but if we analyse the
content and take out those that are general courses, such as General Art
and Design, and those studies which are not totally design specialisms, such
as Practical Archaeology and Stage Management, then we can categorise
the specialisms into three main areas:

- communication design and production
- fashion and textiles
- three-dimensional design

The most obvious thing about the list and the three main categories is that
'Art' is not referred to. This may seem odd to many students, especially as
all the courses are generally studied in schools of art or art departments. It
does, however, emphasise a main distinction which BTEC has identified.
The word 'Art' is synonymous with the 'fine arts' of painting and sculpture.
Since these activities are not considered to be commercial they are outside

the BTEC remit of providing and validating courses that lead to identifiable jobs.

General Art and Design courses are the exception to the rule. Unlike all other BTEC design courses they prepare students for high education, either at BTEC Higher National level or BA level. Because of this there are no BTEC Higher level courses in General Art and Design.

'Art' is, however, a major element in any BTEC design course. Design, in its broadest sense, could be defined as 'the planned shaping of our environment and the things we use'. All artefacts, however primitive, may be said to have been designed, and the people who make them could be called designers. BTEC design courses teach that there is more to design than problem solving and making things, however. Design must also improve the quality of life and create things that people will want to live with.

Designers who have studied on BTEC design courses, therefore, have all the qualities attributed to the artist: the ability to exercise visual judgement, a good eye for detail and a good sense of form and colour. In the past such people might have been known as commercial artists or industrial artists, but today they are generally categorised as designers.

Communication design and production

This area of studies covers careers in the communication industries: advertising, printing, publishing, film making, etc. The courses BTEC offers in this area are as follows:

Graphic Design/Typographic Design/Printing
Advertising Design
Information Design
Photography
General Illustration
Technical Illustration/Technical Communication
Industrial Modelmaking

Packaging
Display/Display Design
Exhibition Design
Film/Broadcast Vision and/or Sound
Video
Audio Visual Design/Learning Resources Technology
Information Technology Design

As you can see, such studies cover two- and three-dimensional design and create environments as well as products. They all, however, have a common aim: to communicate ideas and feelings through words and images in the most effective, efficient and visually pleasing way. Many art students have traditionally opted for these subjects, particularly Graphics, because they appear to be art and drawing subjects that can lead to lucrative jobs. Art and drawing are common elements of every design specialism, however, and there is a lot more to designing than being able to draw well.

You will find that graphic design and related design areas are changing radically because of the introduction of new technology. Today's designers are expected to be able to use computers and other technical equipment, as well as to be proficient in the traditional design skills of drawing and layout.

'Graphics' or 'graphical communication' are familiar terms in secondary education for describing elements of the Design and Realisation and Design and Communication GCSE programmes. This often leads students to think that Graphic Design is the natural course to study at college. This may not always be the case, however, because the skills you learn in CDT subjects at school may be more relevant for other design subjects, such as Industrial Design.

Graphic Design/Typographic Design/Printing/Advertising Design/Packaging/Information Design

These studies are concerned with communicating ideas, information and publicity, through words and images. Most of the designs are eventually printed, either as stationery, publicity material, posters, packaging, books, magazines and newspapers. Designers in this area not only have to organise the layout of words and images in exciting and effective ways, but also need to have the technical knowledge and skill to take artwork through to print production.

Recently, with the growing use of computers, computer graphics, computer typesetting, word processing and desk top publishing, students are now required to develop basic computing, keyboard skills and an awareness of relevant technology.

Possible job outlets include not only working for graphic design consultancies, which deal with anything from corporate identity to logo design and packaging, but also working with printers as paste-up artists, for a publishing house on book or magazine design, in an advertising agency as a visualiser or designer, in information graphics on sign systems, and in the marketing sector of industry on packaging or publicity material.

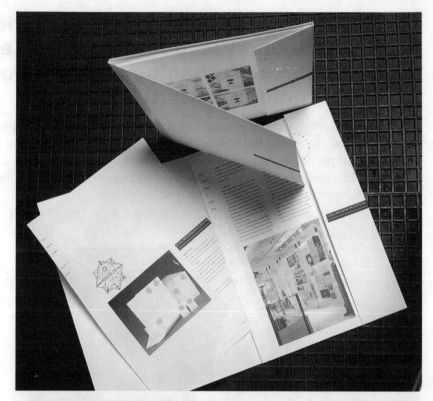

Film/Photography/Broadcast Vision and Sound/Video/Audio Visual/Learning Resources Technology/Information Technology Design

Although most art schools and art departments have photographic facilities, few can afford the range of equipment needed to sustain a specialist course in photography, video or film making. Such courses rely on students learning about the art of image making and the development of skills and

techniques by 'hands-on' experience of equipment. This can be very expensive.

There is obviously a great deal of specialist knowledge and technique development needed to achieve technical consistency and professionalism, but students also have to have a high degree of visual awareness.

Photography has been an intrinsic part of communication for many years. It is used for illustration, recording information, creating a visual impression or giving impact to publicity material. The job opportunities, therefore, range from the obvious, high-profile jobs such as fashion photographer or press photographer, to advertising, industrial, scientific or medical photographer.

Film and video production is expensive. It is also a very effective form of communication, however, that is being used more and more for education, training, publicity and marketing. Consequently there are opportunities for employment in this area outside the union-restricted industries of national film and television.

General Illustration/Technical Illustration/ Technical Communication

At first glance illustration would seem the natural choice of subject to study if you were good at drawing and wanted a career that would exploit these skills. The quality of professional illustration is exceptionally high, however. The competition for work, which is usually on a freelance basis, from magazine and book publishers, design consultancies or advertising agencies, is extremely keen.

There are, however, more specialised areas of illustration you could work in. These include scientific (e.g. biological, medical, zoological, botanical) illustration, cartography and technical illustration. With such specialisations a natural aptitude for drawing is not enough. You will also be expected to be aware of specific technology, understand technical language and develop some specialised visual communication skills.

Industrial Modelmaking

Modelmaking is sometimes categorised under three-dimensional design, but we have included it in this section because it is a very valuable form of visual communication. Not only does a model give added impact to a design, it is also an essential medium for evaluating how things feel or appear when looked at from all angles. Most industrial design consultancies use modelmakers, therefore, as part of the design process at visualisation and design presentation stages. The same can be said of architects, interior designers and motor car manufacturers.

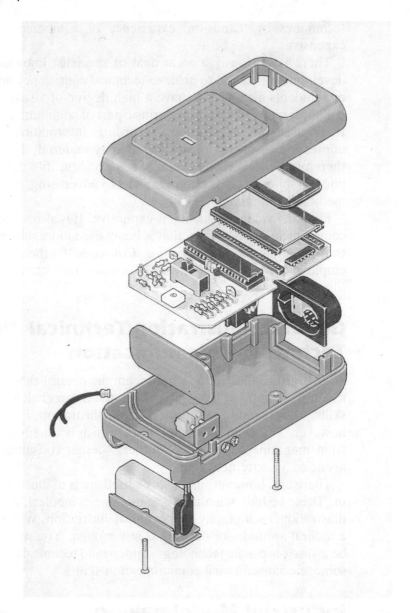

Modelmakers can also find work in preparing models for museums, television, video and film-making industries or models for advertising purposes.

Modelmakers obviously need good manual skills. They also need a range of communication skills in order to interpret engineering drawings and architects plans, for example, and technical knowledge to select appropriate materials and construction methods.

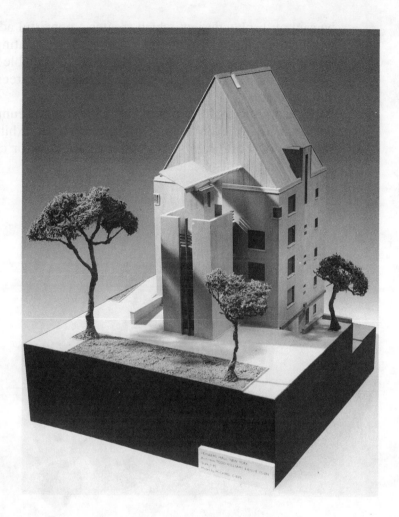

Display/Display Design/Exhibition Design/ Museum Design

Like industrial modelmaking, this area of design is sometimes categorised in the three-dimensional design area either as separate specialisms or grouped with interior design and called 'spatial design'. We have included the specialisms under communication design and production, not only because we feel that they are very important communication media, but also because this is how BTEC categorises them in its guidelines to colleges (see Appendix).

Exhibition designers do not only have to display objects and images in exciting and visually pleasing ways, they also have to explain why such things are being exhibited, tell a story or put over a message. The same can be said of display design, which creates a powerful advertising image for a product by relating it to an environment or associating it with other strong visual images. Designers in this area have to be able to visualise displays, create images from merchandise and construct three-dimensional settings and structures.

If you are successful you could get a job in a museum, in exhibition design consultancies, or even in large industries that use exhibitions for marketing. In addition, most large stores employ designers for creating shop window displays and point-of-sale material.

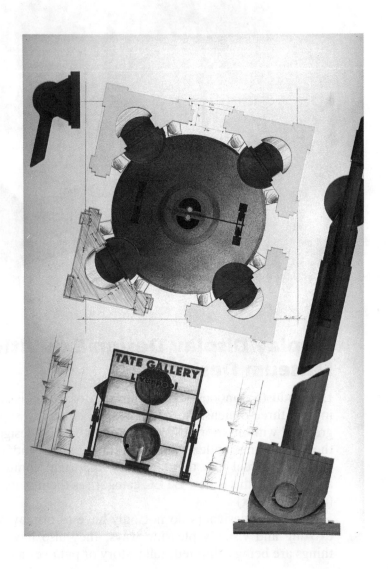

Fashion and Textiles

To say that fashion designers create the clothes we wear, and textile designers the fabric that clothes are made from, would only be half true. Fashion designers are not just concerned with clothes, and textile designers are not just concerned with fabric. Fashion pervades many products and areas of manufacture, and fashion designers could be employed to design clothing accessories, sports products, or even car interiors.

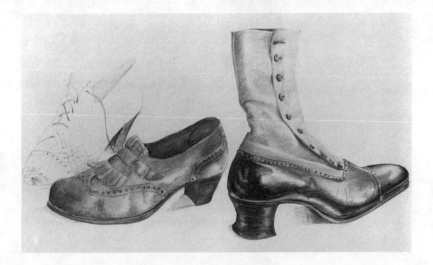

The same diversification is true of textile design. No longer are textile designers content with designing cloth for the fashion industry. Textiles are made up into curtains, bed clothes, furniture coverings and even carpets. The skills such designers have for creating patterns, co-ordinating decoration, and using shapes and colour in exciting ways can extend from textiles to other materials, such as wallpapers or laminated work surfaces. In the car industry textile designers are being asked not only to design the material that is used on the car seats, but also to co-ordinate all internal fittings.

Fashion design and textile design are different disciplines, one creating products from materials and the other creating the materials. They do, however, complement each other and are so reliant on each other that often courses combine the two disciplines. They do this in a variety of ways to provide designers for a range of industries and occupations. These courses include:

Retail/Manufacturing/Freelance/Small Workshop Operations
Fashion with Textiles/Fashion with Marketing
Textiles with Fashion/Textiles with Marketing
Fashion/Textiles Design/Promotion/Consultancy/Management, etc.
Fashion/Textiles/Colour Forecasting/Design Servicing

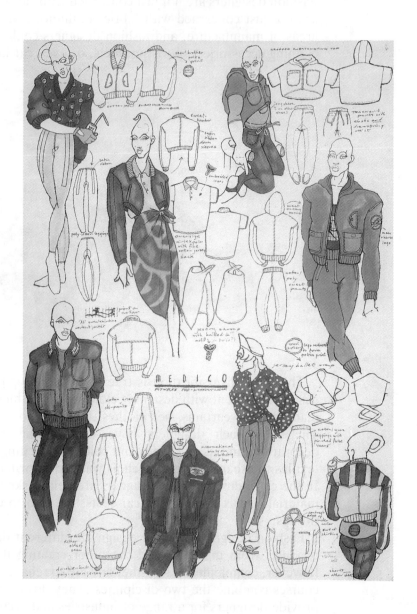

As with other design specialisms, the blend of creative ability, technical knowledge and skills is very important if the designer is to make an effective contribution to the fashion and textile-related industries. Students have to learn about the technical aspects of fabric/materials and clothing production as well as developing their creative ability, communication skills and fashion awareness.

Not all fashion and textile designers will find employment at the designing end of the industry. There are not enough jobs and few students achieve the degree of fashion awareness that some people have for being in-tune with fashion trends and anticipating change. There are jobs, however, for trained fashion designers in the manufacturing side of the industry, in marketing, buying advising, or in the actual production of clothes and fashion products.

The Clothing and Allied Products Industry Training Board has researched the needs of industry until the end of the century. It forecasts that there will be many developments in the manufacturing side, and concludes that all courses in fashion and textile design should also train people for production and marketing.

Most courses in this area have also responded to the introduction of new technology into the industry. As well as developing traditional skills and knowledge, you will, therefore, be expected to have experience of computer aided design and manufacturing systems (CADCAM).

Three-dimensional design

This area of study features a range of specialisms in which skills, knowledge and working approaches may be very different. It is, in fact, an umbrella title to cover the design and production of three-dimensional products and environments. It includes the following areas of study:

Industrial Design
Furniture Design
Product Design (jointly validated by the Boards of Engineering and
    Design at BTEC)
Ceramics
Glass
Silversmithing and Jewellery
Interior Design/Spatial Design
Theatre and Film Set Design

It can also overlap with other areas to include exhibition design, display and packaging.

As can be seen from this list, the specialisms fall into two main groups: *Product Design* and *Environmental/Spatial Design*.

Product Design includes product design, industrial design, furniture design, ceramics and glass design, jewellery and silversmithing, and packaging design.

Environmental/Spatial Design includes spatial design, interior design, theatre and set design, exhibition design and display.

Each of these areas is different and not only requires different technical facts to be understood and used, but also different design, communication and visualising skills.

Industrial Design/Product Design

Both these titles are different ways of saying the same thing. Both disciplines, are concerned with the designing and shaping of mass-produced products. Both try to blend function and form in order to create products that work, can be made, are commercial and are visually pleasing. Both disciplines, therefore, need to consider products in relation to users, makers and society in general. And both disciplines need designers with a high degree of technical knowledge combined with commercial and social concern.

The difference between the two specialisms is generally in the approach and historical roots of each. Industrial design has evolved through the art school system and the designers are primarily concerned with the appearance of the product and the way it relates to the people who use it. Technology is needed to make the objects real, workable and capable of manufacture.

Product design has evolved from the engineering sector and its designers are primarily concerned with the function of products. Styling and ergonomics, for example, are needed to make the products more pleasing to look at and make them more marketable. Quite often though, given these different approaches, the general aim of both specialisms is very similar.

Although most people would agree that products should look good as well as work, the task of persuading industry to use industrial/product designers has been long and difficult. Gradually, however, more job opportunities are being created in design consultancies as well as in industry. If you became an industrial/product designer you could be designing anything from medical goods to domestic lighting or refrigerators.

In the past this area of design has had difficulty in attracting students because of the technical input necessary. Now, however, with the growth of CDT in schools, it is becoming more popular and more colleges are including it in their prospectuses.

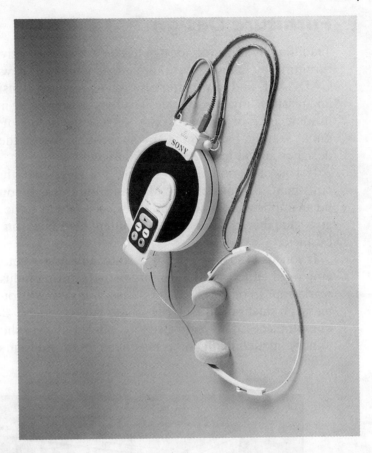

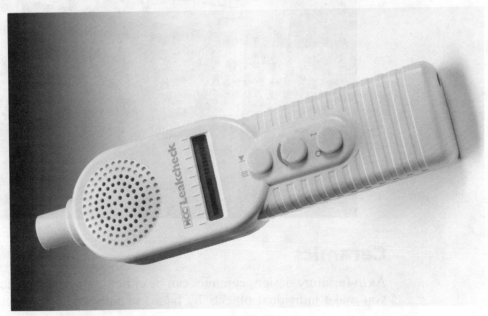

Furniture Design

Traditionally, furniture design has been the craft activity of making wooden furniture by hand. With the introduction of new technology such as CADCAM, and new materials such as medium density fibreboard (MDF) and plastics, however, the design element is growing in importance. Indeed, in some areas of this specialism, such as the design of office equipment and public seating, there can be no distinction between the roles of the furniture designer and industrial/product designer.

If you are good at woodwork, and feel that there is a role for the craftsman, do not despair. Most furniture design courses recognise this to be an important element and allow such talents to be developed. They also give guidance on possible job outlets or advice on setting up your own business.

If you are studying or want to study a furniture course, you could later be employed either in the furniture manufacturing industry or in a small craft workshop. In one you could be designing domestic or contract furniture for mass production and in the other you could be designing and making one-off pieces. There are also job opportunities in showroom management, joinery, modelmaking or as part of an interior design or architectural team.

Ceramics

As in furniture design, ceramics can be either craft-based, which means that you make individual objects by hand, or industrial, in which objects are

mass produced. Ceramic objects can range from the purely decorative or sculptural to functional sanitary ware.

BTEC design courses in this subject usually recognise the range of possibilities and give students a broad experience of both craft and industrial methods of production. Topics covered on such courses include kiln construction, kiln firing, glaze preparation, mould making and casting techniques, as well as developing traditional manual skills. In many courses there is also a strong business and marketing element in order to prepare you for setting up and running your own business.

In some colleges glass is offered as an additional specialism since it is closely related, both in the sort of things that are made and in the methods of production.

Career opportunities can either be found as a craftworker in a small studio pottery producing hand-made objects, or as a designer for mass or batch production in industry, producing anything from tableware, such as dinner services, to sanitary ware, such as sinks and lavatories.

Silversmithing and Jewellery

This is the most decorative range of products covered in this section, and the concentration is mainly on craft-based techniques and skills. There are opportunities, however, to try out not only traditional jewellery skills and materials, such as precious metals and gems, but also experiment with new ways of making things and new materials such as plastics or fabric. Studies obviously concentrate on developing craft skills and learning about the materials and processes which have traditionally been used, but there are also opportunities to learn about mass-production methods for such products as costume jewellery and cutlery, and for examining the wider aspects of the subject.

Once again, as in the other mainly craft-based subjects, opportunities exist not only for working in industry but also for working by yourself or in partnership with other craftworkers.

Interior Design/Spatial Design

Interior designers are concerned with the design of living, working and leisure spaces within buildings and structures. They create environments that are pleasant to be in, have ambiance or atmosphere, and fulfil the function for which they have been made. They do this not only by working with the designers of the building, the architects, creating enclosures that are interesting, pleasant and functional, but also by selecting and arranging the objects in the space. They are concerned with selecting the furniture, fittings, floorcoverings, etc. and co-ordinating the essential elements of

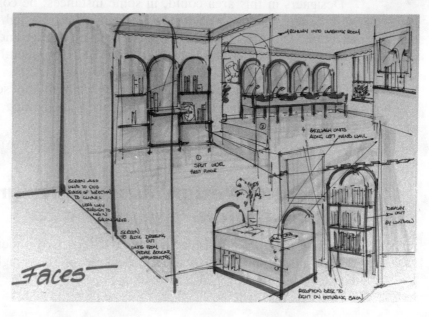

light, colour, texture, shape and form. To be an interior designer is to be a member of a team, because interior designers work with architects, builders, quantity surveyors and even graphic designers.

Although interior designers have to be aware of technical details such as structural constraints, it is also important that they understand and appreciate the practice of, and legislation relating to, associated activities such as architecture and building services. In addition they must be aware of the products available for use within interiors and be able to source and cost such materials and objects.

Job opportunities are to be found in interior design consultancies, working on shops, hotels, offices, cinemas, etc., in an architectural practice or in the architects' department of local government. Interior design training can also be a step to getting jobs as buyers or technical sales persons in shops, stores, or specialised services such as kitchen design centres. You could also become a purchasing advisor in a government agency such as the Crown Suppliers.

Theatre and Film/TV Set Design

There are a few BTEC courses available which specialise in theatre and film set design, developing those skills that create the dramatic settings for stage, film and television productions. Like the interior designer, the theatre designer uses the elements of light, colour, shape and form to create the right mood, complementing actors, costumes and the production itself.

Designers in this area could, in some instances, be concerned not only with the sets, but also with costume design, stagecraft, lighting and property selection. This is especially the case in smaller theatre and film companies. In larger companies these activities are more frequently carried out by separate specialists and rigidly controlled by unions.

Job opportunities range from scenery painter and set constructor to period researcher and technical management of lighting, as well as set or costume designer.

Exhibition Design/Museum Design/ Display Design

All these design specialisms have been categorised under 'communication design and production' by BTEC because of their high communication content. See pages 17–24.

Other areas of design

As you can probably see, it has been very difficult to categorise specialisms, and even though BTEC has attempted to do this, it also recognises that there is a high degree of overlap between some subjects and others. Some colleges have exploited this overlap and created inter-disciplinary or even multi-disciplinary courses.

Such courses recognise the need for teamwork in large design consultancies producing 'total' design concepts for shops and industry. In these companies designers do not just design products or shop interiors, they create an image for the company through buildings, products, packaging, transport and employees.

Design crafts

As we have seen, many design specialisms, such as furniture, ceramics and glass, have a strong craft element. In these courses traditional manual skills are developed and you are helped not only to pursue design careers in industry, but also to set up your own companies and be self employed. In order to prepare for the commercial realities of life, therefore, BTEC courses in this area place great emphasis on ensuring that you have a good business awareness and understand marketing, taxation, book keeping, etc.

Although it is always possible to develop the craft approach in many of the BTEC specialist design courses, there are also general design craft

courses. These allow you to develop particular crafts alongside others who may have different preferences, sharing such common elements as Visual Studies, History of Art, Complementary Studies, and Business Studies. In such cases the range of potential crafts is extensive and could include:

Furniture Making	Blacksmithing
Pottery	Bookbinding
Glassmaking	Silk Screen Printing
Musical Instrument Production	Fabric Printing
Weaving	Stained Glass
Jewellery	Knitting
Silversmithing	

BTEC places emphasis not only on the commercial aspects of such crafts, but also on the visual qualities of the objects the craftworker creates. You must have, therefore, good visual awareness and a sense of form, shape, colour, texture and pattern, as well as being manually skilful.

Activity 4

Because there are so many design specialisms, those listed above are not described in depth, and the specific skills, knowledge and awareness that each area requires from its designers have not been examined. The best way for you to get this information is to find it for yourselves. Choose *three* design disciplines, preferably from different categories, and find out more about each one.

You can get this information from books, magazines or videos, but you will find that the best method is to talk to someone. Look through *Yellow Pages* and see if any designers are listed in your locality, or go to a company to see if they use designers. This will provide you with first-hand, up-to-date information on the subject, and allow you to hear personal preferences and viewpoints.

When you have researched the different specialisms, create a 'careers information sheet' for secondary school pupils. This should contain pictures of the type of work each type of designer would do, the jobs that are available, what sort of training and education are necessary and where they can study.

Are there any skills that are common to all the design specialisms you have chosen? List these common elements and try to put them in an order of importance.

Summary

In this unit we have looked at the various areas of design and indicated potential jobs and careers. We hope that this information will be useful and will help you to choose that particular area of design best suited to you. If, however, you are now as confused or even more confused than you were before, do not despair.

BTEC design courses, as you will discover in the next unit, are all structured to develop a range of similar subjects and skills. These studies are known as 'Core Studies' and are common to all design disciplines as well as each BTEC design course. Because there is this common element, it is possible to delay your choice or even change your course. This is especially useful if you decide that you are on the wrong design course and are worried about future career prospects.

If you have already made your choice of design career, do not think that it is a waste of time finding out about the other areas of design. In most design activities nowadays you will have to work with designers from other specialisms, either in design teams or as sources of specialist expertise.

Do not think that you can do everything yourself. It is only when you know about the specific skills and knowledge needed for each specialism that you begin to understand why specialists exist and how useful they are.

UNIT 4 Core Studies

Are there skills or design knowledge common to *all* design specialisms? If so, what are these common elements?

> In this unit you will:
>
> - find out about Core Studies;
> - understand why every design course includes them on the course programme;
> - be aware of the special relationship design specialists have with other design specialists, because of common values, attitudes and skills.

Design is one of the sectors of education that expects students to pass from National level to higher education in addition to specific employment. There are jobs suitable for National level students, such as technicians/ juniors in design or technical salespersons, but these are not common or, in fact, desirable for many students, who usually prefer to study further in order to become fully trained designers with greater potential for employment in more satisfying and better paid design jobs.

National level students can progress to BA honours courses as well as BTEC Higher National level courses. BTEC Higher National level students can progress to a final year of a BA honours course or even go to an MA course. Success depends not only on the piece of paper that proves you have reached a certain academic level, but also on your portfolio of work. This will allow potential employers or higher education interviewers to see and judge your talents for themselves.

As you have seen in the previous unit, there are a lot of different design courses to choose from. These range from the specialist to the general, and from the common to the rare. Some of you may have done a lot of research into the type of design course best suited to your individual aspirations and talents. Many of you, however, probably applied to the course in your local college, restricted by travelling and living costs. You may feel, therefore, that you have been channelled into an area of design that does not suit you.

Do not worry. BTEC recognises the need for flexibility in design courses. It has made sure that all the courses, even those that are very specialised, have common elements of study. These elements are transferable from one course to another and are useful for all types of designing jobs. BTEC calls these common elements *Core Studies*. It has issued directives, called *Guidelines*, to every college and every BTEC design course, describing what they are, how important they are, and insisting that they be included in every design course programme.

It is these Core Studies that this unit, and much of this book, will concentrate on. You will find out what they are and be given the chance to develop the skills and knowledge that they cover in the project work. If you want to read for yourself what BTEC says about Core Studies you can find this out in a BTEC booklet called *BTEC Guidance – Core Studies in Design Courses* (see Appendix).

You will probably find that this booklet is not very easy to understand, because it uses educational 'jargon'. This is because it has been written for educational specialists by educational specialists. For this reason we will try to explain what the document says.

BTEC lists the following Core Studies.

- Visual Studies
- Historical and Contextual Studies
- Business Management and Professional Practice Studies
- Communication Studies
- Common or Transferable Skills

Visual Studies

These are the studies that develop your creativity and sense of visual judgement. They allow you to experiment with and observe what can be done with form, structure, shape, colour and texture. By doing such studies you should be able to identify and select elements and combinations of elements that are not only exciting but also blend with each other to be visually satisfying.

Such studies are recognised by BTEC, design lecturers and professional designers as being an essential way of developing that awareness which designers believe to be peculiar to their profession.

It is this awareness that not only allows designers to solve problems, but to do so in a different, creative way. It enables them not only to participate in the logical evolution of a design, but to create new forms and fashions that are exciting and stimulating because of their uniqueness. And it develops an ability and confidence to predict trends and convince others to share this vision.

Such awareness is difficult to define and even harder to understand. It is not luck or a natural talent. It has to be developed like every other skill or understanding.

There are no rules for getting it right, since breaking the rules is an essential element of some of the best creative design. It is only through experimentation, being able to stimulate comment, listening to comment, analysing comment, evaluating personal ideas and modification of ideas, that you can develop the experience of knowing which rules to break, when you should break them and by how much.

Visual Studies develop such awareness. They help you to build up your own ideas and experiment with some of the concepts and individual skills that may set you apart from 'run of the mill' designers. Such individualism could also make you a highly sought-after designer. Even designers and lecturers do not know why some designers are more 'creative' than others, or what the secrets of success are. What they do know is that there are situations and areas of study that have proved to be useful ways of stimulating and developing creativity. Visual Studies is known to be one such way.

Of course, not all of you are going to be, or will want to be, leading designers. It is not the intention of BTEC that you all should. One of the successes of the BTEC design courses is that they have recognised that design operates at many levels and that there are jobs and careers at each level, all of which can be very satisfying. At whichever level you intend to get a job, you will find Visual Studies essential. Some of the experimentation you will find yourself doing may seem to be in contrast to, rather than integral with, other elements of the course, especially if you are on a specialised design course. Other things you will find obviously relevant.

Drawing, for instance, is a major part of Visual Studies and, as we have said already, drawing is one of the skills that is of paramount importance to the designer.

You will not only develop drawing skills by visualising ideas in project work, you will also have to do observational drawing. In many cases this will include life drawing, a tried and tested way for developing manual skills, such as line control, the use of shade and tone, and the application of a range of media. It also helps the development of thinking and analytical skills.

Good observational drawing is not just a demonstration of manual dexterity. A drawing can show that you understand how form is structured and can communicate this understanding effectively and efficiently in two dimensions. If you want to do a good drawing, you do not just make lines, marks, tone and shadow. You have to examine, analyse and understand what you are drawing. You have to experiment with ways of translating the form into a two-dimensional drawing that people can understand and is visually pleasing.

Many students find observational drawing not only useful for developing such skills, but also mentally stimulating. Design is, after all, about creativity, problem solving, thinking up new ideas. You will find that you have to 'give out' a lot during the design process. Observational drawing, like other elements of the Visual Studies programme, will allow you to 'absorb' ideas, to be curious, to experiment and 're-charge' your mental batteries.

Content of Visual Studies

We have already said that life drawing, observational drawing and other forms of drawing, such as design sketch sheets and renderings, will be a part of Visual Studies. This will not only be the work that you do in the design studio or life drawing studio, it will include your personal sketch book, work you do at home, and other forms of visual reference.

Such reference may not be drawings. It could be models, or it could include photographs you have taken or found in magazines. You will find it very rewarding, especially as you are developing your own visual awareness and judgement, to select images that stimulate you and pin them up for all to see. Surround yourself with them. They are a form of personal reference and can promote comment from others.

What you choose to select, and why you choose certain images, is an important part of your visual education. The way you develop your visual experience and react to the comment of others will prepare you for the time when you will have to defend your own designs later in your career.

In Visual Studies you will find out about the rules of design and the conventions of visual communication. Whether you do this through personal observation, experimentation or set exercises, these studies aim to expose you to as many visual tricks, constraints and realities as possible.

You will become more aware of the rules and conventions that exist. You will also discover why they exist and how they can be used effectively.

Project 1:   Part 1

You are required to produce a 'mood sheet'. An example of such a sheet is shown below. It could be a selection of images, colours, words and shapes that blend to create a certain mood or image. The way they are presented on the page also reflects this image, and the composition of the sheet is visually pleasing.

The theme for your mood sheet is to be 'sport and the nine-year-old child of today'. Your selection should show clothes, products, colours and images that show that you have researched this theme and have reached some sort of conclusion as to overall patterns, shapes and colours. Imagine that you have been asked by a designers looking at sports clothing to do this research and present it in a way that would appeal to such a child.

The mood sheet should be mounted on an A2 piece of card.

You will learn about visual rules, such as perspective, shadow and tone. You will understand why our brains translate rules into reality, and have a chance to try them out for yourself. You will also learn the rules of basic design, understanding and using colour, line and form to enhance your visual communication skills and the objects you design.

You will experiment with colour and combinations of colour, tone, shadow, shape and form. This will help you to discover potential components for good design and stimulating composition.

You will analyse why certain elements create emotions, suggest things like speed or serenity, or have become conventionalised to represent purity, danger or femininity.

Project 1:   part 2

- Select a small portion of your mood sheet and draw a rectangle 100 × 80mm on it. Then draw the images within this rectangle four times full size so that they fill a rectangle 400 × 320mm.

- Re-draw this image and represent the tonal qualities of the original by using black, white and greys.

- Re-draw the image yet again and select a range of colours that suggests old age and immobility.

- Choose elements of your drawing and produce a repeat pattern using these elements in an exciting way. Select colours that would be suitable for wedding gift wrapping paper.

- Finally, imagine and draw the wrapping paper wrapped around a present. The shape of the form should suggest what has been wrapped up.

Summary of aims of Visual Studies

- To give you extra sources of visual reference and stimuli.

- To help you to develop visual judgement.

- To develop your curiosity.

- To develop your creativity.
- To develop your individualism.

- To give you an understanding of why, when and how colours, shapes, forms and textures are used in designing.

- To give you an understanding of why we have adopted certain conventions to represent objects and images when drawing.

- To give you the opportunity to experiment with and use different media and methods of visual communication.

Historical and Contextual Studies

BTEC describes these studies as: 'the historical and social context from which students may develop an informed and critical awareness of art and design, including the specialised activity concerned.'

Historical Studies

Looking and learning from history can provide you with an important source of visual reference. Most of your visual reference will be the things you see around you – contemporary history. These studies will expose you to many more images from the past, from other countries, and from other cultures.

You will see designs that are exciting not only because they are new, but because they have stood the test of time. These designs have a 'classic' beauty that reflects a deeper meaning to design.

You will look at these designs, analyse them and evaluate them. More importantly, you will be informed of the opinions of others regarding their good and bad features. You will be given guidance on generally accepted views of good and bad design. These views you will have to consider if you are to produce designs that appeal to others as well as yourself.

Contextual Studies

The context in which designers design is important, and the lessons of the past are particularly useful because of the retrospective analysis that has already been undertaken. In such studies you will be led behind the scenes. You will become more aware of the way that politics, society, economics, fashion and social change affect what is designed and the way that it is designed. You will see that change not only affects one specialised area of design but all areas.

You will become more aware of the relationship between the design disciplines, between design and architecture, and design and fine art. This will expose you to trends and movements in the other areas that may have influence on your chosen specialism. It will also make you conscious of the effects that society, commerce, industry, technology and even politics have on design. This is preparation that you need if you expect to shape the future.

This may sound grand, but as a designer you could be responsible for such change. Design is, after all, not just about responding to change and designing for today. Many products may take years to develop and manufacture. The designer has to predict change, predict trends and be aware of the pressures. Only when a designer has such awareness can an informed prediction be made.

Since the designer can predict and influence change, another aim of Historical and Contextual Studies is to remind you of your social and moral obligations. You will then design products that not only please you, the manufacturer, or the buyer, but also everyone that may be affected by your design. This could include society in general and even future generations.

Designers like to think that this social awareness is embodied in their professionalism. They apply it not only to the design of products that are harmful because they physically injure or are harmful to the environment, but also those that create visual chaos and upset the visual balance of the environment because they are ugly.

You will find that Historical and Contextual Studies will not only ask you to consider and discuss thought-provoking topics, it will also ask you to make decisions and state your opinions verbally or in writing. Designers usually prefer to communicate through drawing and other visual media, so you may find difficulty in doing this. If you want to fulfil the changing role of design, however, you must be able to write as well as draw.

Activity 5

- Select a building in your local town that you find visually attractive. Make some drawings of it. Look at the details, the proportions of windows and doors, etc. Include as much information as possible about the building, writing notes on your sketches.

- Find out more about the building, the architect who designed it, the builder who built it, the period it was built in and the reasons for building it.

- Decide what you like about the building and why you like it. Compare it to other buildings that you do not like as much.

- Present your ideas and opinions in a 1000-word illustrated report.

Summary of aims of Historical and Contextual Studies

- To give you extra sources of visual reference.
- To help you develop critical judgement and visual awareness.
- To improve your ability to write and talk about design.
- To give you guidance in analysing images and artefacts.
- To make you more aware of the relationship between different design specialisms.
- To help you develop a sense of social responsibility.
- To make you aware of the factors that promote the need for design.
- To help you develop your own design philosophy.
- To make you more aware of contemporary design and designers, so that you can appreciate their work and suitability for potential employment.

Business Management and Professional Practice Studies

An essential element of any BTEC course, whether it is in design, catering or engineering, is that the students will be preparing themselves for a job. Every design course, therefore, has to ensure that students are familiar with the realities of commercial life as well as being creative and skillful.

Being commercially realistic is very important for every designer. The only way that we can make a living is by designing things that people not only like but can also afford.

Business Management and Professional Practice Studies has several elements. One of these is knowing how industry, business and commerce relate to the designer. You will learn how things are made, how things are reproduced in industry, what is possible and what is not possible. You must understand what can be afforded, what cannot be afforded and what contributes to the final cost of the product.

You will also learn about the way the designer manages the business of designing. This covers the relationship of the designer to industry, the relationship of the designer to a client, the stages into which a design job can be divided, and the cost of design. You may also learn about the problems of running your own business, how to keep your accounts in order, how to cope with taxation and what legal considerations must be understood.

Finally, you will learn about the way industry generally works, how industry is structured, what factors determine the price of products, and the relationship between the designer and industry. Designers have to consider all these factors. All BTEC courses have to introduce students to such aspects if they want to establish the commercial reality that the profession and industry demand.

In many design courses, especially the specialist courses, you will learn about commercial reality through the project work. Some of these projects you may even do in collaboration with local industry. This way you will be able to experience the constraints of industry for yourself as well as be told about them.

You may find these things out during the project briefing. You may find out by asking questions during your research into the project. It is probable, however, that you will learn most by making mistakes and proposing the impossible in your sketch sheets. This will stimulate feedback, comment and advice from your lecturers and specialists. In every case, you will be made to think about commercial realities as well as creative possibilities.

Collaboration during project work is not the only way that your course might introduce you to industry. Many courses organise trips around design consultancies and factories to show how designers work. By doing this you will see for yourself the differences between a designer working in the design or development department of a large company and a designer working in a design consultancy.

You will become aware of the relationship between design and the other areas of industry, or the designer and the client. You will begin to understand that design, like other professions, has to be properly managed to be effective, and that industry expects certain standards from the design profession.

Knowing about the relationship between designers and their clients is known as *professional practice*. To teach this some courses use the services of the Chartered Society of Designers, the body that represents professional designers. Such studies may concentrate on the introduction of design procedure and standards of professionalism, or they may be more detailed and prepare you for self employment.

If you are in a specialism that expects many of its designers to run their own businesses, you will have to know what is expected of the designer, how to draw up a contract, how to charge for your services, how to protect yourself legally, basic taxation and bookkeeping.

Working as a designer in industry presents its own special problems, and BTEC courses will prepare you for these as well. You will learn about the structure of industry, the way it is divided into departments, the way these departments are managed, the way departments relate to each other and the way they might relate to you, the designer.

You will become aware of how cost effective industry has to be, how much design and development costs, how much investment and tooling costs and how much overheads, such as marketing and management, cost. You will have to know about all these things if you are going to design products that can be made and will sell at a profit.

Activity 6

There is no better way of learning about business and commerce than experiencing life in industry for yourself. A period of work placement may be organised for your BTEC course, and this activity is not supposed to replace but supplement it.

With the co-operation of your tutor, try to arrange a visit around a factory or an organisation which uses your particular design expertise. It would be useful if the company had a design department, but do not reject companies that do not. You could, after all, arrange a second visit to a design studio.

The main aim of this exercise is to see the role of design is industry and hear the views of the designer and those that use the designer.

Try to get answers to the following questions:

- How much does it cost to manufacture a product?
- Can these costs be broken down into materials, design and development, overheads, etc.?
- How does the company plan and use design and development?
- How does the company use designers?

and, if you are talking to the designer:

- How do you work with the company?
- How much do you have to know about the company?
- Who do you have to present your ideas to?
- Who briefs you?
- Who decides what products need to be designed?

Use a tape recorder to present a short verbal report of your findings. This can be in the form of a live interview with a representative of the company and the designer, or a summary of your views and findings.

In 1984 BTEC launched an initiative called 'Design by Experience'. This was a series of seminars devised to persuade industry to take on young designers and contribute to their education and training. As a result of this initiative many BTEC design courses now include a period of work placement during the two-year programme. It is quite a common scheme at Higher National level and gaining in popularity at National level as well.

Do not think that you will get a design job for your period of work placement. It is supposed to introduce you to the way that industry and the profession works, so you could find yourself in a variety of jobs. You may not even be expected to work – just observing and doing a college-devised project may be enough to give you the necessary experience of commercial life.

Summary of aims of Business Management and Professional Practice Studies

- To make you more aware of the role of the designer in industry.

- To show you how much design costs and how this relates to the cost of products generally.

- To help you to find out about your professional responsibility to your client, the manufacturer, the person buying your product and all the people who might be affected by your design.

- To introduce the business of design and the standards that the profession expects from its designers.

- To introduce legal problems that you will have to consider when you become a practising designer.

- To make you more aware of the developments and changes that are affecting design and industry.

- To help you to adapt to, respond to, predict and manage change.

Communication Studies

BTEC describes these studies as being 'the communication process, emphasising the importance of spoken and written communication in the precise exchange of information and ideas.'

You may find this confusing, but it does illustrate how difficult it is to separate all the elements that make up design. Designing is a blend of so many elements that we frequently have to cross reference and repeat ourselves. Not only will you see communication skills referred to in this section and Common Skills, you will also come across it in Visual Studies and Design Studies.

Communication is not the only element of design that is repeated like this. When you look at Common Skills in the next section, you will realise that these are not only specific skills to help you fit into the world of work, but also essential skills for designing and project work generally.

You will notice that BTEC, in its Guidelines, emphasises the importance of written and spoken communication. This is sometimes overlooked by art and design students, who frequently use only visual communication skills, such as drawing, to explain ideas and generally express themselves.

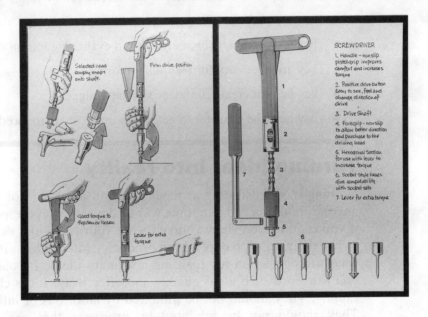

You will have to develop your writing and speaking if you want to be an effective designer. You will need to talk to people to get information. You will need to explain ideas. You will have to interpret technical information and understand technical 'jargon'. And you will have to write letters as part of the business of design.

Industry expects such proficiency. It does not, however, just stop at drawing, reading and writing. There are many other methods of communication you should consider and try to use effectively: photography, video, numbers, foreign languages, computer images and even body language.

Communication skills are essential for the following reasons:

- They help to resolve imaginary ideas and turn them into reality.

- They allow you to criticise, refine, modify and develop your ideas.

- They help other people to understand your ideas, comment on them or accept them.

- They stimulate more ideas.

- They help you to understand what is required of you.

- They are necessary for getting information.

- They are necessary for analysing and evaluating information.

- They are necessary for recording information.

- They help to create confidence in the designer.

- They help the designer to get things made or reproduced.

Turning ideas into reality

Nothing is so frustrating as having a good idea and not being able to tell anyone about, record it in some way or develop it. It is especially frustrating if you cannot even show yourself what your ideas and designs look like.

The designer's job depends on producing lots of ideas. It is important that ways are developed for realising imaginary ideas. It is also important for you to record such ideas quickly and effectively. Ideas change and evolve rapidly. They should not be inhibited by laborious or inflexible processes. They should not be inhibited by processes that are seen as ends in themselves.

Drawing or sketching has proved to be one of the most effective communication methods for the designer. Even sketching can have its drawbacks, however, if the drawings are considered as 'works of art' and do

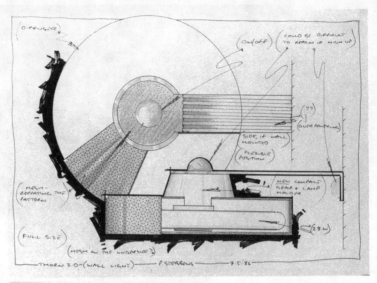

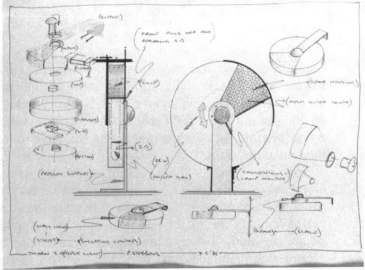

not stimulate a free flow of ideas. In most areas of design, therefore, you will be encouraged to draw as much as possible. You must develop your drawing skills to a point at which you 'talk' and 'think' with your pencil, marker or brush.

You must learn not only to draw quickly but also accurately. If your drawing does not justify the image in your mind you can get depressed or decide to change your ideas. Make sure that such ideas are realised to their full potential by improving drawing skills and understanding how to 'construct' objects and ideas in the drawing.

Sometimes you may find that drawings are not the most effective way to

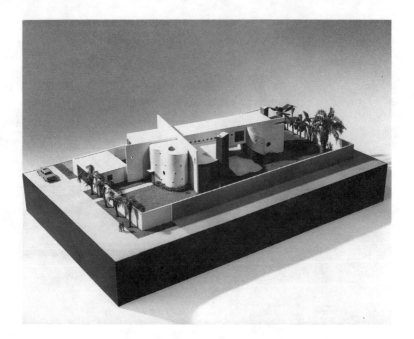

realise ideas, and you may have to develop other methods. Modelmaking, for example, is especially useful in some of the three-dimensional design areas. It is only when you make models that you can get a true sense of scale or find out if it is the right size or shape for someone to hold, get in, sit on, use or operate. In these instances you will have to learn quick and accurate modelmaking skills.

You must also develop writing skills so that you can record other elements of your ideas and designs, and remind yourself of things that cannot be recorded visually or are difficult to draw. Such information might be the name of the material which something is made of, the reasons for a detail, the method of manufacture or even recording a comment.

Sometimes, indeed, you may want to record things that even words, drawings and models cannot convey, such as a mood or a feeling that you want your design to be part of. In such instances you might have to select a combination of images that you have either made yourself or found in books and magazines, and mix these with words and colours. You may even try to extend this by using video and adding sound to enhance the image and mood that you wish to recreate.

Criticising, modifying and developing ideas

It is only when ideas are out of your head that you are able to analyse, modify and develop them. You can either do this alone or in conjunction with other people. Getting ideas generated by a group of people is known as 'brainstorming'. It uses words and discussion to create a range of possibilities from the totally absurd to the probable and possible. It is rather like the game of 'word association' that you played as a child. This game could generate logical thought processes: boy, girl, woman, etc. It could also stimulate less obvious sequences: boy (buoy), sea (see), glasses, etc.

When speaking these words the connection is less obvious than when they are written. Writing communicates that connection more obviously and creates yet another form of stimulus. Drawing adds yet another possibility for stimulating ideas, because people can interpret shapes and drawings in more ways than they can interpret words. You have only to experiment with the game 'ink blots', asking people what a random ink blot is a picture of, to see the variety of suggestions that are offered.

As soon as you communicate your ideas you will stimulate comments and suggestions from students and lecturers. Do not be put off by this. It is a useful aid to learning. The more feedback you encourage, the more ideas you will get and the more you will be able to modify or develop ideas in a positive way.

You must never stop showing people your ideas through fear of comment and criticism. All designers have to show their ideas. All designers get criticised, and one of the best ways of learning is by making mistakes and responding to constructive criticism.

Understanding other people

So far we have talked about communication skills as if their only purpose is to inform others of your ideas or to realise your imagination. We have considered communication only as 'sending' messages. It is also about 'receiving' and 'interpreting' messages, however. This is equally important if you are to get information, interpret information or even be told what tasks you must do.

There are two different forms of communication, *direct* and *indirect*. In direct communication both the sender and the receiver can see or hear the other person. It is, therefore, possible to get confirmation that the message has been understood. This might be a blank look, a nod of agreement or a question for clarification. If we cannot see or hear the other person, however, we must send our messages through a *medium*. This is indirect communication.

Before we can send a message we must have the skills to put it in a form that other people can understand. These skills are called *encoding skills*. To send a letter you must be able to write. Writing is an encoding skill. Even more important is that the person receiving your message has the necessary *decoding skills*. Reading is a decoding skill. When you are trying to

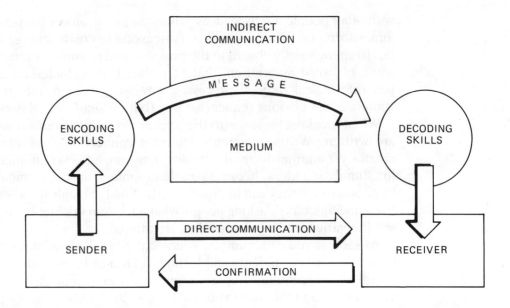

communicate your ideas to other people, you have to know what decoding skills they have before selecting an appropriate medium for communication. When you are the receiver, however, you cannot rely on the sender knowing what decoding skills you have.

Many of the specialists who you will seek advice from or be briefed by will have their own language or 'jargon'. They might even have their own form of drawing 'jargon', such as engineering drawing using orthographic projections. You will be expected to understand this language. Specialists will take a poor view of your design abilities if they have to stop and explain everything to you.

During your course you will be exposed to as much of this language as possible. This will prepare you for interpreting advice and information. The more you understand, the more you will be accepted as a designer. Always ask if you do not understand anything. It is better to ask now, when you are a student and people expect you to ask questions, than to wait until you are a professional designer. Having said that, even in employment you will still be learning. It is better to continue to ask if you do not understand something than to make design errors. Some of the best design solutions begin from apparently stupid questions that stimulate different trains of thought. Get used to asking questions now.

To demonstrate that you do understand the specialist jargon that you will be exposed to, you may have to write letters, summarise the design briefs or write reports. Gradually, through such exposure you will find yourself not only understanding the jargon, but also using it yourself.

Creating confidence in yourself and your design ability

People get more and more confident that you are what you say you are if you can talk their language and demonstrate the skills that designers are expected to have. Specialists not only use jargon and different drawing conventions for communication of ideas, they also use them to test people. They have more confidence in those who can 'speak' and understand their technical language.

The same can be said of designers. They accept those who can speak the language of design. They specifically look for skills, such as drawing skills, in other designers. Drawing is not only a form of communication, therefore, it is a symbol of the profession.

Drawing is a symbol to industry as well as to other designers. The designer is not only employed to solve problems like an engineer, builder, or printer, but is also employed because of his or her aesthetic awareness and ability to produce visually pleasing things. Many people do not have the same degree of visual judgement as the designer. They have to take the designer's word that the designs have such qualities. For some designers this is easy, because they might already have a reputation for producing good design. For others it is not so easy.

Visual judgement is, however, associated with 'Art'. Art is associated with drawing and pictures. Presenting the client with effective and well-executed artwork does not only communicate the idea, it also communicates confidence, competence and professionalism.

You will be encouraged throughout your course to think about both the conscious (informing about ideas) and the unconscious (creating a confident image) aspects of communication. You will have to develop not only good drawing skills, but also neat lettering. You will be asked to look at your spelling, and how you lay out and compose your sketch sheets. You will gradually develop and blend all of these aspects to create the 'designerly image' that you will require to generate confidence from others.

As part of this image building you may also be asked to look at yourself. You will have to assess your personality, the way you dress, the way you talk and listen to other people, and the general impression you create. You may not think such details are important now while you are enjoying the lifestyle of a student, but you will be surprised how important employers consider them to be.

To help you assess such things you may be given mock interviews. You may also be asked to put yourself in an employer's or client's shoes to consider their viewpoint.

Activity 7

Get a colleague or someone in the second year of your course to present a design to you. Ask this person to show you his or her drawings and explain the designs.

Analyse this presentation using the following checklist and give your colleague a grade of either good, very good, exceptional or not good enough.

- Has the person communicated his or her ideas and design? Have you been told what it looks like, how it will be made, printed or produced? Have you been told what size it will be?

- Have you got the impression that this person knows what he or she is talking about? Does this person know about technical constraints, cost, marketing potential, etc.?

- Do you think this person is a good designer? Has he or she produced a good design? Do you have confidence in this person?

- Do you think this person is as good or better than other colleagues?

Write a short report on the presentation. Summarise in your own words everything this person has told you about the design. If you do not understand anything ask for clarification. If your colleague has forgotten to tell you anything, point this omission out so that he or she can improve.

Summary of aims of Communication Studies

- To help you to realise your ideas and designs in order that you and others can evaluate their potential.

- To stimulate comment, advice and suggestions that will help the development or modification of your ideas and designs.

- To help you get your ideas accepted.

- To help you get your ideas and designs made or reproduced.

- To give you and others confidence in your design ability.

- To enable you to ask for information or advice.

- To enable you to understand what people tell you when you seek advice or information.

- To enable you to understand technical data.

Common Skills

To many of you the word 'skills' only conjures up being good with your hands. You will think of drawing skills as being the expertise with which the artist or designer can use a ppencil. You will think of woodworking skills that craftsmen use to make furniture or other artefacts in wood. BTEC, however, uses the word 'skills' to define mental as well as manual skills. These are described in a set of BTEC Guidelines called *Common Skills and Core Themes*. They include:

- self development
- learning and studying
- self management and
- organisation
- working with others
- communicating
- information seeking and analysis
- using information technology
- identifying and tackling inter-disciplinary problems
- numeracy
- practical skills
- skills associated with science and technology
- design skills

If you analyse this list you will see many of the skills you would use when designing and solving problems. They are, however, useful for all students on whatever course they may be studying. They are not just for design students. Skills such as communicating, information seeking, analysis and problem solving need not only apply to the design of a product. They could apply to planning a meal or deciding on the best place to site a grocery shop.

Design skills, on the other hand, actually ask everyone, not only design students, to think about the design of things. They must consider such factors as safety, cost effectiveness, aesthetics and social values.

It is useful to know that many of the skills you are working so hard to develop are useful in other professions and jobs. For this reason they are often referred to as *transferable skills*. You can use them in a wide variety of jobs and they are very important, as you will find out when you undertake a period of work placement. You will find that your design talents do not make you employable. Employers also look to see whether you are punctual, are committed to the job, have initiative, can work in a team, can work unsupervised, and whether you fit in with the people who work with you.

Common Skills are included in your course programme to remind you and your lecturers that you are being trained and educated as a person as well as a designer. You will have to live and work with other people who have not had the same design education as yourself. You will have to work in teams and share skills. Common Skills will make you more effective in such situations.

Activity 8

Try to interview a range of people to see what they feel are the most important skills or abilities that people should have in employment. You need not just talk to designers, and you need not just talk to employers. Talk to employees, factory workers, business people, lecturers and other students.

When you have as many views as possible try to list the skills and put them into some order of priority. Compare this list with BTEC's list of Common Skills. Have they chosen the right skills? Have they left some out?

Summary of aims of Common Skills

- They will help you to fit into the world of work.

- They make you more aware of your employment prospects and your own job potential.

- They help you to learn and continue to learn when you leave college.

- They will enable you to be more self critical and able to analyse what you want from life.

- They help you to solve general problems as well as design problems.

- They will make you more aware of the need for skills other than design skills in the world of work and life generally.

UNIT 5 What is BTEC?

What do you gain from being on a BTEC design course? What is so special about a BTEC course? What, and how, will you learn on a BTEC design course?

In this unit you will:

- find out what BTEC is;

- find out why your design course is called a BTEC design course;

- find out how BTEC courses are structured;

- find out why BTEC courses are structured in the way they are;

- become aware of the elements of your own particular course.

Although we have been referring to BTEC, BTEC Guidelines, BTEC design Core Studies, and BTEC Common Skills, we have not yet told you what BTEC is. Neither have we told you why your course is called a BTEC design course.

Perhaps you do not care what your course is called, only if it will give you the education and training you need to get a job, keep a job and have a career.

You may wonder, however, how other people see your course. You may be concerned if employers recognise your qualifications and whether your education and training will be useful.

You may have already realised that the academic award, the BTEC Diploma or BTEC Certificate, is like passes at GCSE level. It is not the passport to success or a job. Employers or interviewers at higher education colleges will also be looking at your portfolio of work and the impression you create during your interview.

Having such an award, however, does establish a high degree of confidence, because its standards are nationally recognised and there are safeguards to ensure that they are maintained.

This unit will look at BTEC and examine how such standards are maintained.

BTEC is an acronym for the Business and Technician Education Council.

This is a national validating council for vocationally-related courses, that approves courses and ensures standards are upheld.

Validation

Validation is the process which BTEC uses to evaluate and approve courses. When a college wants to run a BTEC design course it has to fill in a questionnaire about the college and the course. The questions are:

- Why is there a need for the course?
- What are the aims of the course?
- What will the students learn on the course?
- How will the course be managed?
- How will the course ensure that standards are maintained?
- What resources does the college have for running such a course?
- Who will teach on the course?

Activity 9

Every BTEC course should have a set of validation approval forms. Ask your tutor to show you a copy, read it and try to understand the educational jargon. Then answer the following question:

How do you know that the course is relevant and what steps has the college taken to ensure that there is a need for such a course?

In the design area most courses are devised by the individual colleges. There are no nationally-devised courses like there are in some other subjects. This means that your course is probably unique. It does, however, have to share many common features with other BTEC design courses, because it has to adhere to certain BTEC Guidelines. As we have already seen, each design course must include certain Core Studies and integrate the learning of these subjects through project work.

If you want to find out what subjects you will study on the course you should look at Form A2 *Structure of Course/Programme of Study* in the validation approval document, an example of which is shown opposite.

B/TEC Business & Technician Education Council

June 1987 **Form A2**

Application for Approval

Structure of Course/Programme of Study

- Read the explanatory notes before completing this form.
- Columns marked with an asterisk do not apply to all courses

Centre number **007**

Award Code **04** (see 1.1)

Sheet No. **01**

Name of Centre (or Coordinating Centre) **BTEC COLLEGE OF ART AND DESIGN**

2.1 Sec no	2.2 Type of unit	2.3 Unit number	2.4 Title (maximum 44 characters)	2.5 Level	2.6 Stage or Year	2.6 Unit Value	2.7 Grouped course Approx Total Hours	2.8 Design SS or PSS	2.9 Combination minimum number of units a	b	c	d	e	f	2.10 Units offered at each Centre (s) Centre ref from Form A1 1	2	3	4	5	6	7	2.11 OL DL	2.12 For BTEC use code
01	T		VISUAL STUDIES 1	N	1		180	CS															
02	T		DESIGN STUDIES 1	N	1		360	CS															
03	C		COMMUNICATION	N	1		120	CS															
04	C		DESIGN PROCESS	N	1		120	CS															
05	C		PRESENTATION	N	1		120	PCS															
06	T		TECHNICAL STUDIES 1	N	1		240	PCS															
07	C		MANUFACTURING	N	1		120	PCS															
08	C		MATERIALS	N	1		50	PCS															
09	C		ENGINEERING FUNDAMENTALS	N	1			PCS															
10	T		COMPLEMENTARY STUDIES 1	N	1		120	CS															
11	C		HISTORICAL AND CONTEXTUAL STUDIES	N	1		60	CS															
12	C		BUSINESS AND PROFESSIONAL STUDIES	N	1		60	CS															
13	T		COMMON SKILLS A																					
14	T		VISUAL STUDIES 2	N	2		120	CS															
15	T		TECHNICAL STUDIES 2	N	2		240	PCS															
16	T		DESIGN STUDIES 2	N	2		300	CS															
17	T		COMPLEMENTARY STUDIES 2	N	2		120	CS															
18	T		DESIGN SYNTHESIS	N	3		180	CS															
19	T		COMMON SKILLS B	N																				

EXAMPLE

→ Total Unit Value

Type of unit
A = amended BTEC-devised unit
S = BTEC-devised unit
D = centre-devised-approved
N = centre-devised-new
Z = common skills

Design courses only
T = subdivision
C = constituent topic
I = individual subject

Combinations
E* = Core unit
E = other essential unit
P = optional unit

OL = Open Learning
DL = Distance Learning

Centre notes (eg selection of options)

Combination	DES code	For BTEC use
a		
b		
c		
d		
e		
f		

Application number

Form A2

Continue on additional copies of this form for further units and combinations

This form also shows you the hours that you will have to study each subject and at what stage. The stages are important because you will have to pass one stage before you can progress to the next.

If you want to know why each subject has been included in the course programme you will have to look at another form, Form A5 *Centre-devised Unit/Subject*. This form describes the reasons for including the subject, the content, the way that you will learn the content and the way that you will be assessed.

You may find these documents very boring to read and difficult to understand. This is because college lecturers, like other specialists, tend to use jargon. It will become apparent, however, that the course you are studying has not just happened. The subjects have not just been pulled out of a hat. Careful thought has gone into devising a course that is relevant to employment needs and each part of the programme has been scrutinised to ensure that it fulfils the standards required for BTEC approval.

Moderation

The method by which BTEC ensures that colleges maintain standards while running a course is called *moderation*. You will probably become aware of this process happening when the BTEC Moderator visits the college. This usually happens two or three times a year.

Many students think that the Moderator is there to assess them and give them a grade for the subject. This is not the case. The Moderator may choose to look at your work and may talk to you about it, because he or she is establishing whether the grades that your lecturers have allocated are both fair and compatible with national standards. The Moderator is not checking on you, but on the college to maintain and uphold national standards.

The Moderator will not only be looking at you and your course, but will also have other colleges to look at. This helps comparisons to be made.

Structure of BTEC courses

By now you should feel confident that your BTEC course has been closely scrutinised and is monitored to ensure that it upholds the necessary standards. BTEC also advises on how the content is presented and how it is assessed. Although the content is presented on the forms as a list of subjects, do not expect them to be taught as separate subjects as you are probably used to at school.

The subjects blend together to form the skills and knowledge that designers need, and are only listed separately as a checklist. This ensures that they are covered during your course. Far from being taught separately, they are integrated into projects, just as they would be in real life.

Why are projects used?

Those of you who have studied for GCSE know that projects or course work are a major element of study. You might even take this form of learning for granted and be surprised if we told you that this is a relatively new method. It was only a few years ago that most students were taught subjects by sitting at desks in a classroom and being lectured to.

The problem with being taught only facts, however, is that facts change. We also need to see the relevance of such facts and understand why they are needed, if we are to use them. By doing projects you will learn things for yourself. This will prepare you and encourage you to carry on learning even when you have left college and are working. You will be able to adjust to change.

In school you would have had a project for each subject. On a BTEC design course you will find that projects are used to integrate the subjects. You will learn the necessary skills in the same way that they would be used in real life. This gives them more relevance.

There are other reasons for using projects:

- They are an active way of learning. You will not be forced to listen to facts being quoted at you in a boring way.

- You will understand why certain skills and knowledge are necessary, because you will discover how difficult it is to succeed without them.

- You will experiment and make mistakes. This will help you gain confidence, learn and develop.

- You will be encouraged to find things out for yourself. You will learn how to learn for yourself.

- You will be able to try out skills and use the knowledge that you have learnt.

- You will see how the different subjects relate to each other and why they have been included on the course programme.

- You will see how the subjects blend together in the job of designing.

- You will learn from many people other than just your lecturers or tutor. When you look for information you will usually find more than is needed on the project. You will be able to share this information with your colleagues. If they too share their information with you, you will be learning considerably more than being lectured to.

Types of project

At National level most projects are devised by the course team, which tries to integrate as many of the subjects as possible and cover all of the elements throughout the period of the course. If it is not possible to include some elements in the projects, then shorter tasks are also included.

On some of the more specialised courses you may also find that the course team uses the help of local industry to introduce realism to the project. This can be useful for the following reasons:

- It allows you to experience new technology, equipment and specialist advice that is not usually available in colleges.

- The specification or brief is often more realistic and detailed than a college-devised project. The scenario is more relevant and the design constraints more rigid.

- You will find that there is often more back-up material and specialist advice available to support the project.

- You will meet and talk with people who are not designers and have very different views to yourself. This will make you more aware of the range of communication skills you need. It will also make you more aware of the fact that industry does not just revolve around design, but is concerned with very different problems.

- You will learn that projects do not begin and end like they do in college-devised projects, and that designing is not the beginning or the end of the product cycle. Although you will have to work to strict deadlines, you will find out that different factors can affect your design and alter timetabling.

- You will experience the preferences and prejudices that determine whether you are a good designer or whether your design is worthy of development. You will find that your college lecturers will assess mainly how you design. They will be concerned with how you tackle the problem, research the project, arrive at design solutions and communicate your ideas.

When you meet with industry, however, the product is their main concern. This is what will make money for their company and what they would be paying you, the designer, for. They take for granted that a designer can design. Working with industry, therefore, can give you a more balanced view of how you and your work are assessed.

Some of these things may be confusing. You will undoubtedly get conflicting advice and opinions when undertaking projects. Sometimes 'breaking the rules' pays off and people praise your initiative and flair. At other times a more conventional approach is more effective. Knowing how to tackle different projects, and when to take risks, comes with experience. A range of projects can give you this experience.

There are some lessons that you will not learn by experience. You will also find that there are lectures you will have to attend. You may find yourself undertaking very prescriptive tasks to learn some craft skills, and you will need to have things demonstrated to you. This makes for a very varied course programme.

Project 2: part 1

By now you should know what qualities you need to be a designer and why you were chosen for the course. You should also have a pretty good idea of what your course is about. You should know something about Core Studies and the other subjects that make up your course programme. Finally, you should be aware of how these subjects blend together in the job of designing and how you will experience this blend in your project work.

You are to imagine that the publishers would like to give away a three-dimensional object with each book. This object would illustrate your particular design course, showing the subjects that are to be learnt and the way they blend together.

You have a free choice of what to design: it could be a mobile, a piece of pop-up graphics or an object with sculptural qualities. In each case, however, your design must be interesting, visually pleasing and informative. It should also reflect the 'feeling' of the course.

Because this object is to be given away with the book, it should be designed to be packaged in a box of the same size as the book. Because it will be produced by the publishers, it should use paper or card rather than materials such as metal or plastics.

You are required to present a model of your finished design and all of your sketch and reference sheets. Explain how your design evolved in a short illustrated report.

Summary

The course you are taking has been closely scrutinised by BTEC, and it is looked at regularly to ensure that standards are maintained. These processes BTEC call *validation* and *moderation*.

The course tutors have identified the subjects that you need to study in order to become a designer and listed these in their submission forms to BTEC. They have also had to explain why they consider each subject to be important and what the content should be.

Each subject, although listed individually, blends with the other subjects when the designer designs. BTEC, therefore, uses a similar method of blending the subjects. This is called *project* work. In other BTEC courses this can also be referred to as *assignments* or *programme of integrative assignments* or *PIAs*. It is a useful way of learning about subjects and the way that skills and knowledge are used in designing.

Identifying the content of each subject ensures coverage of each during the course. If subjects cannot be included in projects, you could also learn about them through lectures, visits, seminars or by doing shorter, more prescriptive tasks.

The course programme will be varied to ensure a breadth of education as well as a narrow vocational training.

UNIT 6 How to tackle projects

In this unit you will:

- discover how project work can be divided up into smaller, more manageable stages;

- find out about some of the problem solving/design/communication skills that need to be developed;

- become more aware of why such skills need to be developed;

- find out and experiment with ways of tackling projects.

Do not expect us to give you a magic formula for doing projects and getting good grades, as there is none. There are no right and wrong ways to design. This is the frustrating thing about design, but also the exciting thing as well.

Different projects need different approaches. The circumstances in which they are presented, the people who present them and even the environment in which they are presented all affect the final outcome. Sometimes you will get results by logically sticking to the brief; at other times diversification achieves more.

Knowing how to tackle each project, when to take risks and what to do at each stage only develops with experience. You have to evaluate the way you are working and the results you are achieving as you work. You will be learning by your mistakes and building on your successes. You must always remember, however, to distinguish between good design and good designing, and the part that consistency plays in ultimate success. One lucky successful design does not make you a good designer.

What we will try to do in this unit is divide the project up into manageable stages and analyse the best way of tackling each. These stages may not apply to every project and they may not always be in the sequence described. You will have to decide for yourself if they are applicable or not when you analyse each project. You will make mistakes, and must learn from them. You must analyse each mistake and decide how improvements can be made.

Just as there are different projects that explore a range of subject matter, there are also different ways of using projects. There are college-devised projects, competitions and 'live' projects with industry. There are projects that are prescriptive and others that are 'open ended' and allow you to select the best method of tackling them.

There are projects for illustrating skills or concepts that you have been told about and there are projects designed to make you find out that you need certain skills and information.

If you look at Project 2 part 1 on page 67 you will see that it illustrated many of the elements we had been looking at, but it did not give you any advice on actually tackling the project. That advice you will find in this unit. We feel that it is better to give such advice now, after you have done the project and made some mistakes, because now you will see more relevance in the advice. Let us first look at the way you could have broken the project up into more manageable stages.

Introducing the project

All projects, however different, have to be introduced. The tutors on your course will try to do this in as many ways as possible so that you will gain experience and improve your communication skills. As we have said before, communication is understanding information as well as giving information. Be prepared, therefore, for being briefed by different people in a range of media.

You might be briefed by designers or design lecturers. You might be briefed by people from industry who work in marketing, engineering or accounts. Whoever they are and from whatever sector of education or industry they come from, you can be sure that each will use specialist jargon. They will also have very different ideas about design and the role of the designer.

Sometimes these people will give you a verbal briefing, sometimes they will write it down. Sometimes they will be present to answer questions, other times they will be on the other end of a telephone, or fax machine. Sometimes you will have to find out everything by exchanging letters.

Analysing the brief

The brief tells you what to do in the project. It is important, therefore, that you understand it. If you do not, you must ask for clarification. Nobody will think that you are stupid if you ask questions. They will not think you have much initiative, however, if you try to tackle the project without understanding it.

To make sure that you understand the brief many courses will ask you to rewrite it in your own words. Many professional designers do this when they have been given a verbal briefing. It ensures that both parties have interpreted the brief in the same way, and can form the basis of a contract between the designer and client. It establishes the designer's professionalism from the outset.

Good briefs are usually composed of several elements:

- the reason for the design
- the design constraints
- the work you are required to present
- the timescale for the project

The reason for the design

This is sometimes called the *scenario*. If you are to design for the company, it is usual for them to tell you about themselves. This will include information on what sort of business it is, what sort of products it makes and markets, who usually buys the products, what sort of production facilities are available, and how they use designers.

You should also be told why they want you to design for them, how they decided that design work was necessary, where they intend to use your design and what their competitors are doing.

In Project 2 part 1 we have not told you anything about the background to the project. We have not, for example, told you anything about the publishers. This is because it is an imaginary project. We have, however, told you that limitations in production facilities mean that your design will be made of paper or card. We have also suggested that the maximum size for each component will reflect the size of the book.

You could also have deduced from our brief that, as it is a give-away product, it should be inexpensive. The price of the book could give you a guide to approximate production costs.

The main thing that the brief told you was that the purpose of the product was to help explain your course in a simple, effective and visually exciting way. We also gave you some of the key elements that we expected your design to illustrate:

- the subjects that you must study
- the way that you will learn the content of the subjects
- how the project work blends the subjects together in a realistic way.

In some instances, especially in the more exploratory projects you will get, the brief may be a statement on the aims of the project. In this project, for example, we could have said, 'the aim is to test whether you have understood the book so far, and can prove that you have by interpreting it in another, visually exciting way.'

Unfortunately you do not have the opportunity to question us about the brief. This might have led to some interesting developments that we could not have perceived. We have assumed, for example, that the design would be something that could be given away with the book. Your research may have shown, however, that a more effective and appealing way to illustrate the aims of the book might be to change the idea of the book completely.

What the scenario does illustrate, even in our simulated version, is that there are primary and secondary reasons for needing a design to be produced. This is not always obvious and you may have to ask more questions, but it is very important that you distinguish the prime initiating factor from the secondary reasons. It would be unfortunate if, for example, given a long list of design considerations for a toy, you did not know that the main reason for re-designing the product was because of its bad safety record. A design solution that fulfilled all the other design criteria but could still be considered unsafe would not be a satisfactory solution.

Design constraints

The *constraints* are all the factors that you must consider when designing. These could be:

- the way the design is to be made
- the way the design is to be printed, etc.
- the material in which the design is to be made
- the cost of the final product
- the market at which the design should be aimed
- safety considerations
- elements that are to be featured in the design

It may not be possible to satisfy every constraint, but you should consider all of them while designing, and try to satisfy as many as possible. In some instances the people setting the project may have just listed constraints without considering their importance. It is possible, however, that some are more important than others. Try to find out.

In Project 2 part 1 the design constraints could be listed as follows:

- The size of the product must be no larger than the size of the book.
- The design must illustrate your design course and the subjects that you will learn.

- It should be visually exciting.
- It should be effective.
- It should be three dimensional.
- It should be cheap to produce.
- It should be easy to assemble.
- It should appeal to students on a BTEC National Diploma design course.

Method of working

When you are set a project at college you will probably be told what work you must show and when you must present it for assessment or criticism. Your lecturer or tutor will help by dividing the project up into stages just as we are doing in this unit. Later, when you are employed, you will not get guidance like this. You will have to judge the situation and select the most appropriate method for tackling the project. You will need to know, therefore, as many ways as possible of tackling projects and get the experience to make the right decisions, saving time and money.

Dividing the time up like this not only allows the staff to present a range of alternatives, it also makes projects more manageable. A project could run for a couple of hours to several weeks. It is easy to waste time if you do not timetable yourself properly. It is easy to find yourself rushing at the end of the programme if you have not set times during the project for the completion of smaller, more achievable deadlines.

In Project 2 part 1 all we have asked for are sketch sheets, reference sheets, a report, and a model of your finished design. We have not suggested how you might divide the project up into stages. A typical breakdown might have been:

- Read the book and make relevant notes.
- Produce sketches that investigate possible solutions.
- Select one of your designs and present it as a design proposal.
- Produce drawings from which you can make the final model.
- Make a model and present it for evaluation.

Professional designers frequently break projects down into similar stages. It is useful not only for managing time, but also for ensuring that design work can be evaluated as the project develops and remains economically viable.

If you produced a design for Project 2 part 1 without going through similar stages and completed the project before evaluation, then you missed the opportunity to build in invaluable safety checks and periods when modifications and improvements would have been generated.

Timetable

We could not build a timetable into Project 2 part 1 because we did not know how you or your course tutor would be using the project. In real life, however, a fixed timescale is not only useful but necessary. The time that you take to do a project may not mean much to you now, but when you leave college and get a job you will see the reality of the phrase 'time is money'. You will be paid to design, and the cost of a project can be more than you estimated if you spend too long on it. Once again it is easier to manage time and work to a timetable if you divide the work up into stages rather than expect to calculate the time for the complete project.

At college early projects will be timetabled for you, but as you progress you will be given greater opportunity to manage time for yourself. You will probably be given a timescale for the total project and then be asked to calculate how long you should devote to each stage. Once you have timetabled yourself it is imperative that you keep to the timetable. Failure to do so will mean that you will have to work longer and longer hours as the deadline approaches. You may even find that you have to rush the final stages and do not have the opportunity for giving your design those vital finishing touches.

Activity 10

Imagine that you have been allocated one week or 38 working hours to complete Project 2 part 1. Divide the project up into stages and work out how long each stage should take. If you have already undertaken the project you will know that some stages take longer than others. You can use this experience to make your calculations. If you have not had this experience you will have to make guesses. Check how well you estimated the time for each stage when you actually do the project.

Imagine that you have been asked to present the work to your client at a couple of stages. Work out when such a presentation would be most advantageous and explain this to your client (Ms Smith) in a letter. Suggest a timescale for each stage.

If you took the week as being Monday to Friday, could you suggest a day and time for each stage presentation?

Evaluating the brief

We have already discussed the importance of reading the brief carefully and clarifying anything you do not understand. You will also have to decide:

- Can you do the work in the timescale suggested?
- What information will you need?
- Does the brief ask you to design something that may not fulfil the needs of the client?

Designers are trained to question. There is always the possibility that the thinking behind a brief is so specific that it assumes a solution that may not be entirely suitable. You must always consider this possibility and decide if the brief reflects the client's true needs. Questioning on this point may lead to a better understanding of such needs.

If, for example, we had only stated in Project 2 part 1 that you had to design a card mobile, we would have assumed that this was the best way to illustrate the book. We would have precluded the possibility of other solutions. The brief would have inhibited your creativity and a mobile might be less effective than other give-away products.

Companies often call in outside design consultants to ask the sort of questions that may stimulate a new direction in their company's design and development planning. At other times they use designers to follow specific briefs. You must be very diplomatic, therefore, in your questioning of any brief.

In our brief for Project 2 part 1 we left you free to decide the best way to illustrate the book. We did, however, suggest a couple of possibilities, of which the mobile was one. To reject the idea of a mobile out-of-hand because you want something different is not good policy either. The object does not have to be different – it has to solve the problem. Consider the problem first, decide how the theme of the book can be best illustrated, consider the use of mobiles and our other suggestions, compare these with your own possibilities and select the most appropriate.

We also said that the product should be made out of paper or card. If you questioned us, however, you might have found that we only suggested this because the printing trade is most familiar with these materials. We have assumed that it would be best to manufacture the product within the company. We had not considered the possibility that it could be made more easily and cheaper elsewhere. As a designer you will gain the experience to be able to select the most appropriate materials and manufacturing methods for a design. You will have to use this experience to advise the client if you think that his or her suggestions are not appropriate. Once again, however, you must be diplomatic in giving such advice.

Project 2: part 2

We have reconsidered our stipulation that your design should be made out of paper or card. We would like you to look at the possibility of using other materials.

We have also been persuaded that a more effective solution to our problem could be something that you wear or get involved in as well as look at.

You are asked to look at as many alternative ways of illustrating this book as possible and select the most appropriate.

When you submit your design sketches and mock-up of the one that you feel to be most appropriate, you should also present an analysis of the relevant production costs and an explanation as to why you made such a choice.

In most of the projects that you will do, your brief will ask you to design or re-design something specific. Perhaps you will be asked to design a new product, advertise something or create an environment. In each case it is likely that the need has been identified by the company before using the services of the designer.

More and more, however, the designer's creative talents are being used to think up new products and ideas. This is what we are asking you to do in Project 2. We are not asking you to design a mobile but something that solves a particular problem.

You will find that such problems will be given to you at some stage of your design course to get you thinking in different ways. You could be asked to suggest ways of creating speed or the illusion of speed. You could be asked to show how a vacuum cleaner could evolve into a fish through ten stages. You could be asked to think of a hammer as a method of driving in nails, not a metal head on a handle.

Research

One of the dangers of dividing the process of design up like this is that you will say, 'I have the brief, now I must do some research.' This is not always the case. Research is not always needed. There are different stages when research might be more appropriate and there are many forms of research.

Research is not just getting information from books, catalogues or even people. It can take the form of experimentation, sketching, observing or doodling. You must be able to evaluate if research is needed and what form that research should take. When you have read the brief and understood it, ask yourself what you should do next. Ask yourself the following questions:

- Do you need information?
- What information do you need?
- Do you really need information?
- Do you need the information now or is it best to think around the problem first?
- Is information available?
- Where can you get the necessary information?
- How can you get the information?
- What will happen if you cannot get the information?
- Can you do the project without the information?
- Why do you need the information?

The general rule is that the more open the brief is, or if you are asked to consider concepts rather than actual things, the less likely you will be able to define what information you will need. In such instances it will be better to think about the problem and come up with some ideas before inhibiting yourself with cost, materials or manufacturing constraints.

Follow the rule that the brainstorming activity advises. Think of quantity not quality and let your ideas flow out of your head and onto your sketch sheets.

In part 2 of Project 2 what information do you need before you can start the project?

Do not begin by going out to find the comparative cost before you have some ideas to evaluate. Some ideas might appear to be impractical at first but could stimulate more fruitful chains of thought. You might begin to think about using a decorated T-shirt to solve the problem. Eventually this may prove to be too expensive but you could develop the idea into paper T-shirts, paper clothes, paper hats, masks or even environments that you get inside.

It is probably best to start this particular project by writing about or drawing as many ideas as possible. Set yourself a target of 50 and then increase this target as ideas begin to flow more readily. Do not be critical of ideas. Put every idea down.

In part 1 of Project 2 you were limited to working in paper or card. You could have started this project either by brainstorming or browsing in your local shops to see how manufacturers use paper and card. Both ways of working would have brought results. There are no set rules.

There is nothing like a project to make you really look at things. You will see details and elements that are normally missed in a casual glance. The more you design, the more you will be able to focus on specific details that create that special effect which turns an ordinary design into an extraordinary one. If you are concerned with designing a plastic moulding, for example, you can achieve a lot by looking at the way other designers have used the material and solved similar problems to your own.

Keep looking at things. Keep analysing why some designs are better than others. Keep recording such information in scrap books or sketch books.

Do not think that you have to do research before you start designing. You must consider the needs of each project and seek information only when and if you need it.

If you decide that you need information, you will have to determine what information you need and where you can get it. In Project 2 part 1, for example, you will need to know how you can cut, fold, print and join paper or card at some stage. Where can you get relevant information?

You might go to a printer, but a greetings card manufacturer might be more useful. They would use more of the processes that you need to know about. Try to think of as many information sources as you can. Ask yourself who uses paper and card.

How you get information depends on your initiative and communication skills. The difficult part is getting started. Once you begin to ask questions, the answers generate more questions and provide more sources of reference.

You can get information by a variety of methods. You can telephone, write letters, send fax messages or go to the information source and ask someone directly. All have advantages and disadvantages when it comes to time and cost. As a student you will find it cheaper and more convenient to write a letter, but the time it takes to get information back makes it a very long process. Direct communication, either by telephone or meeting people, is usually the best way of getting information, because you can build on the situation. This way you not only get information but advice or ideas as well.

If you do telephone or manage to talk to someone, you should always plan what you are going to say and ask. It is easy to waffle – confused questions get confused replies. Write down your questions and give some sort of explanation as to why you need the information. This permits people to focus on the issue and give more relevant answers.

When you write a letter, get it checked by someone else before you send it. This helps to ensure that it communicates what you are trying to say in an effective way. Once more, an explanation of the reason for the request for information helps you to get more relevant information.

If you find a useful source of information, take a note of not only the organisation or company but also the person you have spoken to. This is always useful if you need to contact the company again. Establishing such contacts is a vital part of your design training, so why not begin an address book now?

Activity 11

Look again at your design proposal for Project 2 part 2.
What additional information would you need to persuade the publishers that it is a viable commercial proposition? Put yourself in their shoes and ask yourself questions such as:

- How much will each item cost?
- How will it be made?
- How will it be decorated?
- How will it be packaged?

List the sort of information you think you might need and also the source of such information.
How long do you think it would take to get the relevant information?

You can also get information by reading, looking at pictures, looking at products, thinking about the problem, experimentation, analysis or measurement. It is up to you to choose the most effective way of getting the relevant information given the constraints of cost, time and availability.

Never use the need for research as an excuse for not starting to design. If you plan ahead, you will inevitably find that there are alternative ways of developing a design while waiting for information. Sketching out ideas and analysis of ideas is always useful, even if such work has to be modified later to reflect your research findings. You cannot afford to wait and do nothing.

Analysing and evaluating information

If you have thought about information needs and planned your research, you will find it quite easy to evaluate the relevance of the information you get. Analysis and evaluation may not seem important until you discover how much information you actually get when you start asking questions. Some will be relevant and useful, but a lot will be superfluous and confusing. You will find that you have two problems: the first is interpreting data and information; the second is identifying and prioritising relevant information.

Interpreting information will get easier as you become more experienced. You will gradually acquire an understanding of technical knowledge and the communication skills to interpret the 'jargon' and technical language used by specialists.

Identifying relevant information is mainly about using your common sense and checking off the information you have gathered with your identified information needs.

Whatever information you get, select and keep that which is relevant to your present project. You will need it to find out more about whatever you are to design, for reference during the project and to support your design presentation.

Other, more general information you could use to build up your own reference library. This could save you a lot of time in future projects. Be sure, however, that you keep technical information up-to-date. Old information is not only useless, it can be very misleading.

Getting and developing ideas

The essence of design is being able to get and develop ideas. You will, therefore, spend more time doing this than anything else. You will be learning how to get ideas out of your head. You will be finding out about the way ideas stimulate more ideas. You will be learning how to select promising ideas for further development and refining such ideas into a realistic and visually pleasing design proposal.

There is no magic way to design or to get and develop ideas. You have to learn to design by doing it, by making mistakes and getting experience. How successful you are will not only depend on how inventive or creative you are. It will also depend on the fluency of your drawing skills. These encourage the flow of ideas, stimulate chains of thought, encourage comment and advice and give you the confidence to experiment. You will be prepared to make mistakes. You will learn from such mistakes. You will develop your design experience.

Regrettably we cannot give you much advice on how to get ideas. The way that you think and the associations your brain makes will depend on you. We can advise you to realise your imagination at all cost, develop the skills to communicate your ideas and do not be afraid of criticism. Look upon criticism as a constructive activity, listen to others, analyse what they say and draw your own conclusions. Look at design details as well as grand concepts.

Evaluating ideas

When students are learning to design they often start by thinking that their first idea is marvellous. They then develop this idea until someone suggests another chain of thought. Gradually, with the development of skills, ideas flow more quickly. They can flow and flow. Students do not know when to stop designing. It takes experience to know and recognise a good design, select that design, and develop it. Alternative designs, produced as part of the design process, are not meant to confuse you, but to convince you and others that your chosen design is the best.

Like analysing and evaluating information, it is always useful to make a checklist to judge your design against. You must be careful, however, not to put too much emphasis on individual elements at the expense of the overall blend that is achieved. You must also be aware that seemingly insignificant details can make a mediocre design outstanding.

Once more experience is invaluable. You will only develop this experience by listening to comment on your work and making comparisons with your contemporaries and other designers. This is the purpose of the criticism session or 'crit' at the end of many of the projects. It is an important element of design courses as it is a way of using the work of individuals to explain many aspects of design.

At these sessions all the students will put up their work for comment by the lecturers. Such comment is not just personal criticism but pointers for the whole group. It is a way of establishing standards by example.

The 'crit' is especially useful for promoting an awareness of visual standards that are difficult to define or explain any other way. Such standards have to be shown and discussed to be understood. This method illustrates that these standards are not hard and fast rules but depend on circumstances. A range of work can show when these standards work and when they do not.

The more you become aware of the standards that others use to judge good and bad design, the more you will be able to use such criteria in your own assessment of your work. This will develop from assessment of design at the final stages, such as the design presentation, to an on-going assessment and evaluation of ideas as you design. You will find yourself eliminating some ideas and modifying others as you draw them or think of them.

To help you make this constant evaluation of your design work, your lecturers and fellow students will talk to you, comment and give advice as you are working in the studio. This is why it is important to take advantage of working with others instead of just doing work at home by yourself. Listen to such comments and learn about what people like and dislike. Such awareness will be invaluable if you are the only designer in a company and have to make your own decisions and be critical of your own work.

Activity 12

Professional designers evaluate their designs against experience, but they also have a mental checklist based on their original brief. Produce a similar checklist for Project 2 part 2 and try to evaluate whether your design successfully answers the problem.

- Does the design tell us about the BTEC design course and the subjects that are studied?

- Does the design show the blend of such activities?

- Does the design look balanced, reflecting the balance of subjects that are learnt on the course?

- Are any elements not compatible with the total design?

- Could any details be improved?

- Is the total design visually pleasing?

- Can the design be made?

- Could any of the elements of the design be changed to make them easier to manufacture?

- Do other people like the design?

- Can other people understand the course by looking at your design?

- Would it be suitable to give away with the book?

- Can the design be improved?

- Does the work you presented show that you are a designer?

Preliminary design proposals

Every now and again it is worth summarising your ideas into a design proposal. This is especially useful if your sketch sheets reflect a lot of ideas and the one with most potential is lost among your other ideas. Just produce a sheet every now and again that explains your favourite idea more thoroughly. This will help you to evaluate the idea for yourself and makes you more aware of possible design development problems.

Presenting a design to other people

At some time or other you must decide to select an idea that you feel is worth developing into a product and present it to other people for comment. You will have to present it in a way that people will not only understand but also like. You will have to 'sell' your design.

There is no standard way of presenting your ideas. This will depend on what you are designing and what specialist area of design you are working in. It also depends on who you are presenting your ideas to. Generally, however, you might find the following checklist useful:

- Who do you want to communicate your ideas to?
- What methods of communication would they understand?
- What method of communication would they expect from a designer?
- What method of communication would best explain your idea?
- What method of presentation would market your design best?
- What communication skills do you have?
- Should you risk doing something that may be beyond your capabilities or should you stick to methods you know you can do?
- How long have you got?
- Where will you have to present your designs?
- Do you have to transport your work to the place of presentation?
- Do you need specialist visual aids and equipment, and if so, will such equipment be available?
- Will you be present at the presentation?
- Will you be able to talk about your design and answer questions or will all such information have to be presented through your work?
- Should you just show your final design proposal, or should you also show your sketch sheets to explain development?
- How much should you show them?

- Will you confuse them if you show them everything?
- What should you select?

Ask all these questions of yourself in order to do the following:

- Inform the person looking at your design about every aspect of it so that they will understand it and be able to evaluate it.
- Create a good impression by the way your work is presented, in order to generate confidence in you and your work.

To do this you will need to experience presenting different designs in different situations to a range of people. You will need to develop specific design communication skills such as modelmaking, photography, technical drawing, dressmaking, etc. You will have to develop general communication skills such as reading, writing and talking, and you will have to develop 'common skills' such as tact, diplomacy, confidence and resourcefulness.

You may not only have to plan such presentations, you may also have to adapt your presentation to suit changing situations. You will have to use such situations to your advantage. You will not only have to be a good designer, you will also have to be a good salesperson.

Activity 13

Think about how you would present the designs that you did in Project 2 part 2 to the book publishers. Imagine that you will have to take your work to their London headquarters and present your work at 10 a.m. Three people will be present at this meeting and they will expect you to explain your ideas personally.

- What will they need to know?
- What sort of questions might they ask?
- How prepared are you to talk about potential manufacturing methods and costs?
- How will you display your work?

Put yourself in their position and make a list of the things that you will need to know about. Write a short 'plan of action' predicting how your presentation might happen.

Development

Many students think that design and the job of the designer stops after the client has been presented with the design and it has been approved. This may be true of design at college, because it is not possible to fund further development. In real life the professional designer knows that this is the time that real work begins. It is not just a case of communicating the design so that it can be made, it is a continuous process of designing and modification to get the most out of technology, materials and manufacturing methods. Even when things are being reproduced there may still be the need to make further modifications and prepare for the next cycle of design and manufacture.

Summary

In this unit we have looked more closely at the project. We have analysed why BTEC design courses use projects to help you to learn and we have tried to give you some advice on how to tackle them. To do this we have divided the project up into different sections, activities and stages. We have discussed the *design brief* and how it identified *design constraints*, *methods of working*, and a *timetable*. We then looked at how you should *analyse* the brief, find out *information* or do *research*, and why you should analyse and *evaluate* the information that you find. Next we focused on ways of getting ideas, *creativity*, ways of recording ideas through *sketch sheets*, etc., and ways of *communicating* designs and ideas to other people for *evaluation* and *development*.

It must be emphasised, however, that breaking the project down like this has only been done to give you a guide. It is not a formula. If you follow the suggestions blindly and without thinking you will not get the success that you hope for, because this can only be achieved by you using your own common sense, analysing each project as it comes and determining the best way of tackling it for yourself.

UNIT 7 | Assessment

How do you know how well you are doing? How do you know what is expected of you? What will happen if you are not good enough?

In this unit you will:

- find out why you are assessed;
- understand how and when you are assessed;
- find out about the BTEC system of grading.

Assessment is not new to you. You have had assessments throughout your school life and you will continue to be assessed when you leave college and are at work. Sometimes you have been assessed by doing exams, at other times your coursework has been assessed. You may even have had student profiles. These not only assess your work but also you, your character and the way you work.

You have had different things assessed in a variety of ways. You have been assessed by different people with different views and opinions. It is probable, however, that most of your assessments have been made by your teachers and that a great deal depended on the exam and final assessment at the end of the year. You will probably notice quite a few changes in the way you are assessed on a BTEC design course, but, before we look at this process, it is worth considering why colleges need to assess you and you need to be assessed.

Many people are interested in your progress and potential. A good indication of these factors can be the assessment grades. Employers need them as guidance for potential employment. Lecturers need them to identify your strengths and weaknesses and to plan the next stages of your education. Parents and local education authorities might need them for reviewing your progress. And BTEC needs them before you can be awarded a Certificate or Diploma.

Assessments are not just for other people, however, neither are they hurdles to determine whether you can progress to the next stage of your education. They are mainly to help you. They keep you informed of your progress and give you guidance. Assessments are not just marks or grades therefore; they can be comment, tutorials or even advice. They can be quite formal at certain stages of the course, but it is more likely that they will be part of a continuous learning process throughout the project work.

At first you may be reliant on the assessment of your lecturers, but gradually you will be performing the task yourself in preparation for the time when you have not got such a system available to indicate how well you are doing. You will gradually learn to make comparisons with your past work or the work of your contemporaries. You will be analysing the criteria which have been specified in the brief or shown in the 'crit', and you will be judging yourself against the standards of professional design.

Your tutors will help you to assess yourself. They will be commenting on progress as you work, discussing strengths and weaknesses and advising on routes for development. They may even be having formal tutorials with you in order to review your work and the way you are working. You will be asked to look at your attitude, design awareness, commitment and other such aspects that will affect your potential as a creative designer and useful employee.

Assessments do not have to result in your being given grades. You are being assessed all the time as part of the learning process and you should be assessing yourself as well. But every now and again you will find it useful, if the college records opinions of you and your work as grades.

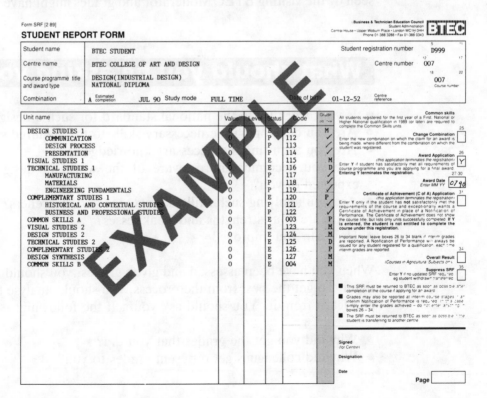

You will find that you do not get just a single grade for the course, but grades for each subject identified on the Course Programme. This will give a better picture to the course team, your lecturers, BTEC and potential employers of your overall strengths and weaknesses than a single grade.

What else are assessments used for?

Assessment grades are not only indicators of your progress, they are also indicators of the progress of the course and the standards of teaching. Your lecturers will be using assessments to see whether the projects and assessments have been used effectively and that you have had the opportunity to learn about those things for which the project had been planned. They will be looking at weaknesses in the programme or the way that projects are planned and managed, and they will be using their findings to plan the input of future projects.

They will also be comparing you and your colleagues to previous years of students and students in similar courses nationally. If they are grading too high or too low in comparison with staff on comparable courses this will be seen by the visiting BTEC Moderator and grades might have to be changed.

What should you be asking yourself?

- Is your work up to the national standard for such a design course?
- Are you developing the necessary skills to the required standard?
- Are you acquiring the necessary knowledge?
- Are you becoming more aware of the world of design and what is expected of you?
- Are you applying such skills, knowledge and awareness?
- What are your strengths and weaknesses?
- How can you improve?

When you have been assessed and given grades, you should not just ignore them. To get the best from the process, you should analyse the assessment and learn from it. You should ask yourself the following:

- Why did you get the grades that you did?
- Why did colleagues get different grades to you?

- Was the grade for the actual piece of work or for the effort put into producing it?
- Do the grades reflect the criteria you were given during the project?
- How do you rate against other design students on other design courses?
- What are your strengths and weaknesses and why?
- How can you improve?
- Are the grades fair?

How important are the actual grades?

You have all probably looked back over the marks and grades that you got in junior school or early in your secondary school education and thought how wrong or right they were. Sometimes grades are a good indicator of performance and potential, sometimes they are not. Perhaps the grades are not as important as the assessment process itself.

One of the factors that will become obvious as you become more aware of the world of design is the lack of interest in academic qualifications. Employers and even colleges will not take qualifications as the only indicator of design ability or employability. They will prefer to see you and your work for themselves in order that they can make their own assessment.

You probably found this to be the case when you applied for your BTEC National design course and went for an interview. You would not have been accepted onto a course just because you had 5, 6 or 7 GCSEs. You would have had to prove to the panel of interviewers that your work was of an acceptable standard and that you have the personal qualities suitable for development into a professional designer. They would have balanced your academic qualifications, standards set and judged by others, with their own criteria for acceptance. It is not that they did not trust your examination results, it was because greater specialisation in further education demands different priorities and different criteria. You will find that this re-assessment is repeated by others when you apply for a Higher National BTEC course, a degree course and even a job.

Do not think, however, that because your work will be re-assessed by others, your present grades do not matter. Colleges and employers have many applicants. They use academic qualifications as a method of initial sorting and final selections. To have a BTEC award gives the employers or college a benchmark of quality. They can assume that those who have the award are worthy of an interview. Those who do not have a similar award are less likely to be suitable.

Similarly, if two candidates perform equally well in an interview, a review of academic qualifications may be a major element in the panel's decision making. Passing your course and getting good grades is desirable, therefore. It is not, however, the only thing that matters. You cannot rely on an award alone to get you a job. No award, not even a BA degree, can promise you that. You will have to be re-assessed again and again by future employers, colleges, professional bodies and clients through your design career.

How are you assessed?

One of the strengths of BTEC courses is that you will be prepared for re-assessment throughout your education and working life. This may be done by a range of different people in a variety of ways, so BTEC asks colleges to use a variety of assessment methods and get people other than lecturers to take an active part in the assessment procedures. BTEC feels that this will not only give a fairer distribution of grades, but also make you more aware of the different expectations and criteria that people measure you against.

You will be assessed by your tutors, part-time or visiting lecturers, colleagues, (what is known as peer assessment), special visitors, employers and representatives of the companies running collaborative projects. You will also be expected to do your own self assessment.

You will probably find it very difficult and most disconcerting to assess yourself, especially when you have to allocate grades. You will become more aware of the problems that other assessors have in defining assessment criteria and deciding what is good or had, what is a pass or fail, or what is a distinction. And through such awareness you will develop those visual judgement and self-evaluation skills that will be so necessary when you are employed as a designer.

Some things you will find easier to assess than others. You may find it relatively easy to assess a piece of work, that has constraints and assessment criteria well defined, but other aspects you will have difficulty with.

In Project 2 you would already have evaluated your design as you were designing. You would have been checking that your design fulfilled the checklist of design constraints and modifying your design as you went along. Look again at the questions you should have asked yourself in Activity 12 (page 82).

Superficially these look very simple questions. Some of them you could answer with a straightforward 'yes' or 'no'. But does this signify 'good' or 'bad'? You could say 'yes' or 'no' to the question of size, but how much does it matter if the design was slightly oversize but exceptionally good in other respects? Even if the design can be made, how much better is it if it can be made more cheaply or easily? Each response gets increasingly difficult as you begin to analyse the question and ignore 'gut reaction'. The problem is that design depends on the blend of all the elements, and the combination determines whether the design is good or bad.

Not only do you assess design objectively, you also use subjective judgement. This is especially the case in determining whether the design is visually pleasing or not. Such evaluation depends not only on rules that can be learnt, but also a general awareness of aesthetic standards that can be developed only through experience.

You will probably find it easier not to consider each criterion separately, but to look at the overall blend that is achieved. In doing this you must recognise that sometimes criteria can be prioritised, assume different levels of importance, or change in importance as they are used in different ways.

You should frequently refer to your original design brief, determine the criteria stated or suggested by the constraints, and analyse why some blends work and others do not. You should learn to be methodical in applying definable criteria but flexible in your response to subjective judgements as well.

Although you may be concerned primarily with your design solutions, you must remember that the lecturers have other concerns as well. They will, of course, be concerned about and highly critical of design solutions because this is what ultimately determines a good professional designer. They will also be analysing how you reached such a conclusion.

They will be looking at and assessing the process of design as well as the final product. The grades that you get for a project, therefore, may be different to what you might expect. Producing a good design solution does not automatically mean that you will get good assessment grades for every element of the course.

When will you be assessed?

Your lecturers will be asking the following:

- Does your design show that you are able to apply the technical knowledge that you have learnt on the course?
- Have you applied the knowledge in an intelligent way?
- Have you built on the knowledge you have learnt, found more information and interpreted it correctly?
- Does your work show that you are able to interpret the brief?

- Have you shown that you are able to think through a problem, propose ideas and select a design for development?
- Have you developed ideas to an appropriate level?
- Have you communicated your ideas effectively?
- Have you presented your ideas in a way that gives people confidence in your design ability?
- Have you managed your time effectively?
- Does your work look like it has been produced by a designer?

In answering such questions your lecturers will be concerned with fulfilling the aims and objectives that have been identified in the subjects that make up the course programme. You must remember that the project is a carefully structured way of integrating all the course subjects in a realistic way. In assessment the lecturers have to identify and separate these subjects once more in order to allocate grades for each.

Many of the things that need to be assessed can be identified in the work that you submit at the end of each project. By looking at this your lecturers will not only be able to assess elements such as design ability or communication skills, but also commitment, time management and your self-learning skills. They will, therefore, be looking at the amount of work you have produced, whether you were able to complete each stage on time, and the way you modified and developed ideas in response to criticism.

Assessment of project work does not give the complete picture, however. For this your lecturers need to consider other methods of assessment. They cannot tell, for example, whether you have initiative, are conscientious or can work with others. These have to be assessed by watching you at work, talking to you or, in the case of team projects, talking to your colleagues.

BTEC design courses do not only have one form of assessment, they have many. They do not only assess the products that you design but the way that you work as well.

When will you be assessed?

The course team would not only have decided why you need to be assessed, what needed to be assessed and how you should be assessed, they would also have determined when you should be assessed. It is difficult to suggest standards for each project, especially in the early, developmental stages of the course. It is more usual to assess at set stages throughout the year. This is often once a term. In doing assessment in this way your lecturers can not only evaluate the separate projects but also your progress and whether you have attained certain levels of skill, awareness or knowledge.

Almost all BTEC design courses are well established or operate in a School of Design which has a tradition of running similar courses. Consequently, the staff are experienced at knowing the standards that students should be capable of at set stages of the course. They can quite often show you examples of other students' work to help you to understand their expectations more clearly.

Activity 14

To help you to see more clearly what will be expected of you, ask several second year students on your course to show their folders to you and explain the projects. Find out when the projects were undertaken and what their grades were at the different assessment stages.

Write an essay on what you see to be the main differences between your work and that of the second year students.

When are you eligible for an award?

If you look at your own course programme as described on Form A2 in the course's Application for Approval documents, you will see what will be recorded on your Diploma or Certificate. In the example on page 94, for example, *Visual Studies*, *Design Studies* and *Technical Studies* are called *subdivisions*. *Communication*, *Design Process* and *Presentation* are all *topics*. You will be graded for all the subdivisions and topics which make up the subdivisions, but only the grades for the subdivisions will be recorded on your Certificate or Diploma. You have to pass each subdivision to be eligible for the final award.

Some courses are structured in a different way. The one illustrated on page 95 is made up of *units*. You will get a grade for each unit and this will be shown on your Certificate or Diploma. Once again you have to pass each unit to be eligible for the award.

You will get grades rather than marks, because BTEC feels that this gives a fairer picture of your achievements, is easier to understand, and relates more closely to national criteria than precise percentages or similar marking systems. There are three possible grades that you can get. BTEC defines these as Pass, Merit and Distinction (see page 96).

B/TEC Business & Technician Education Council

June 1987   **Form A2**

Application for Approval
Structure of Course/Programme of Study

- Read the explanatory notes before completing this form.
- Columns marked with an asterisk do not apply to all courses

Name of Centre (or Coordinating Centre) ___BTEC COLLEGE OF ART AND DESIGN___

Centre number ___007___   Award Code ___04___ (see 1.1)   Sheet No. ___01___

2.1 Seq no	2.2 Type of unit	2.3 Unit number	2.4 Title (maximum 44 characters)	2.5 Level	2.6 Stage or Year	2.6 Unit Value	2.7 Grouped course Approx Total Hours	2.8 Design SS or PSS	2.9 Combination minimum number of units a	b	c	d	e	I	2.10 Units offered at each Centre (s) centre ref from Form A1 1	2	3	4	5	6	7	2.11 OL DL	2.12 For BTEC use code
01	T		VISUAL STUDIES 1	N	1		180	CS															
02	T		DESIGN STUDIES 1	N	1		360	CS															
03	C		COMMUNICATION	N	1		120	CS															
04	C		DESIGN PROCESS	N	1		120	CS															
05	C		PRESENTATION	N	1		120	PCS															
06	T		TECHNICAL STUDIES 1	N	1		240	PCS															
07	C		MANUFACTURING	N	1		120	PCS															
08	C		MATERIALS	N	1		60	PCS															
09	C		ENGINEERING FUNDAMENTALS	N	1		60	PCS															
10	T		COMPLEMENTARY STUDIES 1	N	1		120	CS															
11	C		HISTORICAL AND CONTEXTUAL STUDIES	N			60	CS															
12	C		BUSINESS AND PROFESSIONAL STUDIES	N			60	CS															
13	T		COMMON SKILLS A																				
14	T		VISUAL STUDIES 2	N	2		120	CS															
15	T		TECHNICAL STUDIES 2	N			240	PCS															
16	T		DESIGN STUDIES 2	N	2		300	CS															
17	T		COMPLEMENTARY STUDIES 2	N	2		120	CS															
18	T		DESIGN SYNTHESIS	N	3		180	CS															
19	T		COMMON SKILLS B	N																			

←Total Unit Value

Type of unit
A = amended BTEC-devised unit
S = BTEC-devised unit
D = centre-devised - approved
N = centre-devised-new
Z = common skills

Design courses only
T = subdivision
C = constituent topic
I = individual subject

Combinations
E' = Core unit
E = other essential unit
P = optional unit

OL = Open Learning
DL = Distance Learning

Centre notes (eg selection of options)

Combination	DES code	
a		For BTEC use
b		
c		
d		
e		
f		

Application number

Form A2

Continue on additional copies of this form for further units and combinations

Form A2
[6/88]

Business & Technician
Education Council **BTEC**

Application for Approval
Structure of Course/Programme of Study

- Read the explanatory notes before completing this form
- Columns marked with an asterisk do not apply to all courses

Centre number: 117101

Award Code: 06 (see 1 1)

Sheet No.

Name of Centre (or Coordinating Centre): Nonsuch College

21 Seq no	22 Type of unit	23 Unit number	24 Title (maximum 44 characters)	25 Level	26 Stage or year	27* Unit value	28* Grouped course approx total hours	Design SS or PSS	29 Combination minimum number of units a	b	c	d	e	f	210* Units offered at each Centre (x) centre ref from Form A1 1	2	3	4	5	6	7	211 OL/ DL	212 For BTEC use code
01	D	12345	VISUAL STUDIES	N	1	3·0		PSS															
02	D	12346	COMMUNICATION	N	1	2·0		PSS															
03	D	12347	DESIGN PROCESS	N	1	2·0		PSS															
04	D	12348	PRESENTATION	N	1	2·0		PSS															
05	D	12349	MANUFACTURING STUDIES	N	1	2·0		PSS															
06	D	12350	MATERIAL STUDIES	N	1	1·0		PSS															
07	D	12351	ENGINEERING FUNDAMENTALS	N	1			PSS															
08	D	12352	HISTORICAL AND CONTEXTUAL STUDIES	N	1			PSS															
09	D	12353	BUSINESS AND PROFESSIONAL STUDIES	N	1	1·0		PSS															
10	D	12354	HUMAN FACTORS	N	1	0·5		PSS															
11	Z	12355	COMMON SKILLS A	N	1																		
12	D	12356	VISUAL STUDIES 2		2	2·0		PSS															
13	D	12357	DESIGN STUDIES	N		5·0		PSS															
14	D	12358	TECHNICAL STUDIES		2	4·0		PSS															
15	D	12359	COMPLEMENTARY STUDIES	N	2	2·0		PSS															
16	D	12360	MAJOR PROJECT	N	3	2·0		PSS															
17	Z	12361	COMMON SKILLS B	N																			

← Total Unit Value

Type of unit
A = amended BTEC-devised unit
S = BTEC-devised unit
C = centre-devised—approved
N = centre-devised—new
Z = common skills

Design courses only
T = subdivision
C = constituent topic
I = individual subject

Combinations
E* = Core unit
* = other essential unit
P = optional unit

OL = Open Learning
DL = Distance Learning

Centre notes (eg selection of options)

	Combination	DES code
a		
b		
c		
d		
e		

For BTEC use

Application Number

Form A2

Pass	satisfactory performance in all major areas of the subject or unit as defined by the principal objectives outlined in the course programme
Merit	performance either significantly better than a Pass in all aspects of the subject or unit; or outstanding in some areas with Pass performance in others
Distinction	outstanding performance in all major areas of a subject or unit

Activity 15

Get a copy of your course programme as defined in the Application for Approval document. Look what the course team has said about Assessment Strategy in section 3.5 and in the descriptions of the individual subjects or units.

Check to see if there are any pre-requisites for progression from one stage of the course to the next.

Try to analyse what the documents say and write your own explanation of the assessment system. If you do not understand anything ask your lecturers to explain.

Some courses are divided into stages and you will have to pass each stage before you can progress to the next. If you fail any subject or unit you will have the chance to resit it or do extra work. If this is the case, however, you will not be able to get a Merit or Distinction for this subject. The only grade that you can get for a re-sit is a Pass.

When all the assessments have been completed and the grades determined, your results will be presented to the college's Board of Study and the BTEC Moderator for formal approval. If they are approved, they are then recorded on a BTEC Student Report Form (SRF) and sent to BTEC. This system of checking and approval ensures not only that the grades are consistent with national standards, but also that you have the chance to appeal or make comment if you feel that you have not been fairly treated.

It is important that you resit any unsatisfactory subject or unit before the SRFs are sent to BTEC, as a later submission may mean that you will not get your Diploma or Certificate as quickly as you would like. Passing before July will mean that you should get your awards by September or October. Late submission could mean a delay of several months.

Good luck, work hard, do not be afraid of making mistakes, learn as much as you can and enjoy yourself. Design is, after all, not a job but a career. It is something that you have to enjoy to do well in. Being a design student should be one of the most exciting and enjoyable times of your life, so make the most of it.

Appendix

BTEC documents referred to in text

All these publications can be obtained from:

Publications Despatch Unit
Business & Technician Education Council
Central House
Upper Woburn Place
London WC1H OHH

Design and Associated Studies – Guideline reference 05-010-4

Common Skills and Core Themes – General Guideline reference 80-051-6

Core Studies in Design Courses – Guideline reference 05-030-8

Other BTEC documents

All of these publications are available from the address above.

Teaching and Learning Strategies – General Guideline reference 80-048-6

Assessment and Grading – General Guideline reference 80-069-6

Books that may be useful if you are choosing a design career or a design course

Guide to Courses and Careers in Art, Craft and Design Tony Charlton
Published by the National Society for Education in Art and Design
7a High Street
Corsham
Wiltshire
SN13 OES
Tel (0249) 714825

Design Courses in Britain
Published by the Design Council
Design Centre Bookshop
28 Haymarket
London SW1Y 4SU

Directory of First Degree and DipHE Courses
CNAA Publications,
344–345 Gray's Inn Road
London WC1X 8BP

BTEC Higher National Diploma Courses in Design and Associated Studies
Registration Scheme Booklet
Available from Association of Art Institutions,
Penn House
9 Broad Street
Hereford HR4 9AP

CNAA First Degree Courses in Art and Design Registration Scheme Booklet
(also available from the Association of Art Institutions)

Working in Art and Design by Peter Green
Published by Batsford

Careers in Art and Design by Linda Ball
Published by Kogan Page

Handbook for Art and Design Students by Robin Jesson
Published by Longman

Useful addresses

Business and Technician Education Council
Central House
Upper Woburn House
London WC1H OHH

Art and Design Admissions Registry
Penn House
9 Broad Street
Hereford HR4 9AP

Design Council
28 Haymarket
London SW1Y 4SU

Department of Education and Science
Elizabeth House
York Road,
London SE17 7NJ

Chartered Society of Designers
29 Bedford Square
London WC1B 3EG

Council for National Academic Awards
344–354 Gray's Inn Road,
London WC1X 8BP

Polytechnics Central Admissions System
PO Box 67 Cheltenham
Gloucestershire GL50 3AP